Praise fo

"*Take Action* by Dr. Ann Marie Gorczyca lays out all of the pieces of the treatment coordination puzzle. This book demystifies the patient experience and gives you actionable items you can implement in your practice today for treatment coordination success."

—Christopher Phelps, DMD, CMCT
Author of *How to Grow Your Dental Membership Plan*

"*Take Action: Treatment Coordination for a Successful Dental Practice* is a 'Purple-Cow-Wow!' book. This book stands out from the other books on this subject in a super remarkable way. It's a must read, along with Dr. Ann Marie Gorczyca's three previous books: *It All Starts with Marketing: Beyond the Morning Huddle*, and *At Your Service*. Dr. Gorczyca points out that 'Dentistry is, after all, a business.' You are in sales whether you like it or not, and if you don't have effective treatment coordination, your patients will not say 'yes' to treatment. Reading *Take Action*, I learned a lot myself and had takeaways that I will not only employ in my coaching and consulting but in my own dental business as well."

—Robert M. Pick, DMD, MS, FACD, FICD;
CEO of The Pick Group;
Speaker, Coach, and Consultant, known for creating "Purple-Cow-Wows!"

"*Take Action* tackles tough topics in a straightforward, easy-to-understand manner. Dr. Gorczyca inspires 'taking action' in your practice to achieve optimal practice profitability by perfecting communications, financial systems, cash flow, scheduling, and inventory management. *Take Action* is a must-read for every practicing dentist and dental specialist."

—Maryann Kriger, DDS, Orthodontist,
Co-founder of OrthAzone

"I highly recommend all dental students read *Take Action* by Dr. Ann Marie Gorczyca to understand what it takes to have a successful dental practice. *Take Action* will take your dental practice from good to GREAT."

—Debbie Steidel-Bittke, RDH, BS
Founder and CEO, Dental Practice Solutions

"Sales and dentistry can mix together like oil and water unless you have the right formula. Just as there is more than one right way to prep a crown, there are many effective ways to present and close the new patient exam and start treatment. The only thing that matters is the result. In *Take Action*, Dr. Ann Marie Gorczyca shares her formula for effective treatment coordination. This book will serve as a valuable resource to help dentists and their teams and help them create a positive impact through effective case presentation and effective management of the treatment coordination process."

—Jeff Palmer, Co-Founder Case Acceptance Academy

"Dr. Ann Marie Gorczyca is a successful "hands-on" business owner. In *Take Action*, she shares valuable business knowledge with a continual focus on building patient relationships. Her real-life examples of resolution to difficult business problems, which all practice owners and dental teams face, will enlighten the reader. *Take Action* provides step by step formulas for success and is a must-read written by one of the best!"

—Wendy Askins, MBA
Certified Fraud Examiner, Prosperident

"Dr. Gorczyca has fought many of the battles dentists face in the management of a dental practice. In her book *Take Action,* she offers practical solutions to issues keeping dentists up at night and costing them money. The practical methods and extensive research in *Take Action* teach you ways to change your office inertia to a direction that will make your practice more profitable and a happier place to work."

—R. Kim Bleiweiss, MBA, MEd
President, Lean Dental Solutions, Inc.

"*Take Action* by Dr. Ann Marie Gorczyca describes with contagious enthusiasm the dental sales process. Included are strategies for improving team performance with open-book management. Sales success can be increased by asking the right questions and consistency of follow-up. The most successful treatment coordinators and dentists are highly skilled at sales. *Take Action* offers management strategies you can use to improve new patient starts, reduce accounts receivable, and increase patient referrals. I highly recommend all dentists read *Take Action* and add it to their business acumen library."

—Aimee Muriel Nevins, BS, MS, Coach, Fortune Management

"*Take Action* is required reading for every dental professional and team. This book will help you through each aspect of 'closing the sale,' commit patients to treatment, and move your practice toward greater success. This book leaves no treatment coordination detail unattended; from the potential patient's initial phone call, first impressions, the doctor's role in success, team expectations in a vibrant practice, pre- and post-initial exam communication, financial mastery, understanding statistical benchmarks, and dozens more relevant practice builders. "Dr. Ann Marie Gorczyca presents the material in an entertaining and thoughtful way, ensuring that you and your team will learn treatment coordination strategies and enjoy the process along the way. Intriguing quotes and examples culled from the unique personal experiences of dental and business stars will inspire you to take action. Dr. Gorczyca's outreach to an array of experts will round out your education in every area of patient enrollment. I recommend *Take Action* without reservation.'"

—Nancy Hyman, Founder, Ortho Referral Systems
Marketing Manager, Hyman Orthodontics

"*Take Action* is rich with usable content and ideas easy to put into practice in your dental office. A Treatment Coordinator's roll is **sales.** Period. Dr. Gorczyca has captured this concept in her book and described the actions and tracking needed to make your office's treatment coordination process a success."

—Jill Allen & Associates, Orthodontic Consultants

"Dr. Ann Marie Gorczyca takes a comprehensive approach to the mechanics and psychology of running a successful dental practice. Her attention to detail is supported by years of practice, research, and education. This step-by-step guide should be in the hands of every dental practice owner and manager. Dr. Gorczyca has remained current and on the leading edge of what dental leaders and teams can and should be doing in today's business climate. I highly recommend '*Take Action*' and look forward to future works by Dr. Gorczyca."

—Lisa Mergens, BS, MA, RDH, Executive Leadership
and Team Development Coach

Take
ACTION

Treatment Coordination
for a Successful Dental Practice

DR. ANN MARIE GORCZYCA

AUTHORITY
PUBLISHING

Take Action: Treatment Coordination for a Successful Dental Practice
By Ann Marie Gorczyca

1. MED016090 – Medical: Dentistry - Practice Management
2. MED016000 – Medical: Dentistry – General
3. BUS043000 – Business & Economics: Marketing - General

Hardcover ISBN: 978-1-949642-37-7
Paperback ISBN: 978-1-949642-38-4
Ebook ISBN: 978-1-949642-39-1

Cover design by Lewis Agrell

Printed in the United States of America

Authority Publishing
11230 Gold Express Dr. #310-413
Gold River, CA 95670
800-877-1097
www.AuthorityPublishing.com

To my husband,
Richard J. O'Donnell, M.D.,
a man of action.

CONTENTS

FOREWORD

BY GINO WICKMAN

My book, *Traction*, published in 2011, has helped tens of thousands of owners of businesses of all sizes learn how to gain effective control of their business management systems, including many in the service and healthcare industries. *Take Action*, by Dr. Ann Marie Gorczyca, offers a systematic approach to dental practice management and the treatment coordination processes of daily patient care. Together, the two books are the perfect marriage for helping you run a great practice.

Take Action is a blueprint for the business and human side of dental and orthodontic treatment coordination; it will help you manage your team, increase accountability, and gain traction for office success. Dr. Gorczyca's book offers insights to ensure consistency of systems that you can use as a dental office leader. Her concepts will enable you and your dental team to get a grip on dental business and reduce the stress that comes when your business has a grip on you.

Take Action is a how-to manual. Its evidence-based approach offers ideas for immediate use in your dental office, including practical solutions to overcome common challenges. It's not complicated or theoretical. All it takes is insight, analysis, systems, and team action—the consistent execution of assigned responsibilities to produce change and results.

Dr. Gorczyca shares the vision of the system I created called EOS (The Entrepreneurial Operating System), which goes to the root of all organizational issues—the six key components of any business. They are:

Vision. Everyone in the business must share a vision for success—which goals are to be achieved, and what direction the company is taking. The business can't be about you, or any individual, with desperate, unorganized, thinking. Less is more. The most important long- and short-term goals must be succinct, clear, and known by all. Once known, the directives can be shared by all. As the owner or leader, you must elevate yourself above the business, look down on it objectively, and make decisions based on the shared vision for the long-term, greater good of the company.

Great People. Successful business owners surround themselves with great people. These people Get it. Want it. And Do it. They are eager and capable. They are able to set goals for the success of the organization. Shoot for the ideal in your dental practice. Surround yourself with 100 percent of the right people.

Data. Your numbers are your business score. You can't fly blind. You need objective data. Business numbers reviewed weekly reflect sales progress, cash flow, overhead, and customer ratings. Only the factual information of numerical data can provide the basis for productive discussion and decision-making power. Make everyone on the team responsible for a number. What gets measured gets done.

Issues. Moving forward requires pulling up the anchors holding you back. Ask, "What's holding us down?" The answer is nothing and no one. It's normal to have issues. The sooner you can admit what these obstacles are and view them as a means to solutions rather than as a weakness, the faster you will smoke issues out and resolve them. Calling out issues creates an environment of openness and honesty, creating a high level of trust that in turn produces healthy and functional teams able to follow through on difficulties until resolution. Your practice is not a democracy. It is owned by someone who has taken the risks of business ownership. In business, consensus management does not work, period. Business leaders must have strong will to make the tough decisions for the success of the organization.

Process. Nothing can be fine-tuned until it is first consistent. Clarify your systems. Document your core processes, including your sales process, human resource management, marketing, operations, cash flow, and customer service. Your goal is then to streamline processes. Create efficiencies by simplification and cross-training so that all aspects are self-sustaining. Once processes are set, they must be followed by all. Manage people to stick to the core processes.

Traction. You have no option but to work through the push-back of adherence to systems if you want to have a great company. Accountability, discipline, implementation, and execution are areas of weakness in most organizations. Squarely address the fear of discomfort and gain the traction necessary for business success. Weekly meetings produce a pulse of engagement with the most important common goals. Concentrate on the now. Break down the vision into bite-sized pieces. Start with short-term goals to achieve your long-term goals. Remember, ownership of results includes a date and meetings are the moment of truth for accountability. Start and complete what you have to do. Get everyone on your team fired up and working towards the most important goals for the success of your practice.

The ideas in *Take Action* are not revolutionary. But newfangled hype is the last thing most leaders need in running a dental practice. What's missing in most businesses is the consistency of fundamental processes. Dr. Gorczyca's book will help you anticipate, plan for, and navigate the complexities of treatment coordination in the management of a dental practice.

When leaders of dental practices do not master the fundamentals of business management, the consequences are significant and costly: (1) the owner experiences stress; (2) suboptimal team members drag the business down; (3) time and money are wasted in inefficient and unimportant processes; (4) employees have negative attitudes and do not attend to the most important work; (5) available tools to increase efficiency are not implemented; (6) high performers become frustrated; and (7) the business stagnates and never reaches its full potential.

On the other hand, when leaders practice the fundamentals consistently, the business gains traction: (1) you hire high-performing team members who are "all in"; (2) more productive and important work is done; (3) morale improves; (4) resources are used wisely to grow the business; (5) business management and cash flow is predictable; (6) waste is eliminated and your business is more profitable; and (7) the dentist/owner and the entire dental team experience less stress and higher fulfillment.

Take Action is a solid guide to applying the fundamentals of dental practice management with purpose. Mastery requires total commitment, and gaining traction requires you to implement an operating system. This book will help you to clean up and clean out your dental treatment coordination sales pipeline. It will inspire you to perform system check-ups routinely, which produces continuous improvement.

In short, you have work to do! You have to organize your systems, hire the right people, influence your patients, make tough business decisions, and tackle daily issues that arise in the running of your dental business. Neglecting these processes would be like going to the doctor, being prescribed medication, and then not taking the medicine to cure your health problem. You will need to *Take Action* to correct your own practice system ailments. This book offers you powerful tools to do just that.

Gino Wickman is the founder of EOS Worldwide and the creator of EOS® (The Entrepreneurial Operating System®), which helps leaders run better businesses, gain control, and achieve life balance. EOS Worldwide helps companies implement EOS through a team of hundreds of EOS Implementers and online support. Gino conducts workshops and delivers keynote addresses that help organizations advance together as healthy, functional, and cohesive teams. He is the author of the books *Traction: Get a Grip on Your Business (2011), Get a Grip: An Entrepreneurial Fable (2012),* and *Leap: Do You Have What It Takes to Become an Entrepreneur? (2019).*

INTRODUCTION

*Either write something worth reading or
do something worth writing.*
—Benjamin Franklin

Today is the day to take action toward growing your dental practice. To do this, you will need to welcome a new patient and start his or her dental treatment. Simply put, you need to make a sale.

Treatment coordination is sales. It is getting the patient to "Yes!" in order to deliver the dental services. Yet, we don't talk about our dental offices as having a sales department. Sales is a word which is rarely spoken. Dentists hire registered dental assistants, financial coordinators, and office managers. Ads on Craigslist rarely if ever say, "Job Opening: Dental Salesperson."

Yet, this is exactly what is needed for dental practices to be successful. Not only front desk and financial team members need to know how to make the sale, close the deal, and get to "Yes!" with a new patient, so does the doctor.

I've seen many dentists "unsell" their own dental services. As an orthodontist for over thirty years, I have worked with more than 100 dentists. Cases can be easy, or complex; some can cost $40,000 or more, and can take up to five years to complete. Some dentists get the job done easily: they are easy to work with and a pleasure to talk to, inspiring the trust and confidence of patients and interdisciplinary specialists alike. Other dentists, many of whom are truly excellent from the technical standpoint, manifest a style that deters patients from starting treatment: They go into too much detail, overwhelming the patient; they emphasize what could go wrong, rather than the benefits of treatment; they fill the patient with fear rather than confidence and enthusiasm. Then they shock the patient with the total cost.

We, as dentists, can achieve greater success by planning and implementing a seamless sales process, also known as treatment coordination. Quantification allows us to measure improvement. Focus allows us to perfect our systems. Mastering the sales process leads to less stress, more fulfillment, a happier team, and a more profitable and successful dental practice—and of course, patients receiving excellent treatment!

We are fortunate to have the opportunity to do this work. Smiles change lives. This vision will drive you to deliver high-quality dental services with conviction and excellence. Your passion will lead you to be a lifelong student of dental practice management along the way.

Owning a Dental Business

I have always said that everyone is in sales.
Maybe you don't hold the title of salesperson,
but if the business you are in requires you to deal with people,
you, my friend, are in sales.
—Zig Ziglar

The process of running a successful dental practice is challenging. Being a dentist is a full-time job. Your business is constantly evolving. Team members will change; as will patients, technology, and the economy. We must constantly seek advanced business acumen and management advice in order to flourish as entrepreneurs. Without proper processes, dentists would soon be unemployed. For every dentist, treatment coordination is a critical element of the business management mix.

Even the most reliable, stable treatment coordinator will eventually retire. It is likely you will be training more than one such team member during your dental career. Over my career, I have had the pleasure of working with eight different treatment coordinators: Two were non-performers, three were acceptable, two were very good, and one was excellent. I hope to share what is excellent and a best practice in this book.

Outstanding teams know that every new patient start counts. They know their case acceptance numbers. They fill their schedule with new patient production. They know that case conversion is of primary importance. They put first things first.

Treatment coordination can be easily ignored. In the day-to-day challenges of dealing with emergency patients, paying bills, and dealing with difficult team members and patients, attention on new patient starts can be overlooked. This is not a good situation for any business owner. The onboarding of new clients should be center stage. It is the driving force and engine of your dental practice.

To some dental professionals, treatment coordination actions come naturally. For others, treatment coordination techniques or strategies need to be reviewed in order to acquire the highest degree of new patient conversion, payment, and practice growth. Whether you are a novice or advanced practitioner of treatment coordination, the skills outlined here will be invaluable to the management and success of your practice.

When I was a student at the Harvard School of Dental Medicine, I had the opportunity to study at Harvard School of Public Health in the Department of Health Management and Policy. There, while attending management lectures, I started to understand the importance and broad-reaching effects of dental practice management within the broader healthcare services industry.

It was not until a treatment coordinator quit that I dove fully into the treatment coordination process. I hired a personal coach and started keeping score. Then, I truly understood the input and systems of the treatment coordination process and lead actions for results. Out of necessity, I started doing the treatment coordination role myself. I started to experience the best success I had experienced in recent times. In my first month, my treatment coordination success was 96% in a practice that had previously struggled to make the national treatment coordinator average conversion rate of 69%. I started to experience a tremendous amount of fulfillment by being the driver of my practice's treatment coordination process. My practice became more profitable, efficient, and fun. The team was happier, and I was happier. I think the patients were happier, too!

When I started teaching at The University of the Pacific Arthur A. Dugoni School of Dentistry, we added a treatment coordination lecture to the business management curriculum. It was shocking to find that some students graduate from dental school and specialty residency programs without ever having to convince a new patient to start treatment. These young dentists had never in their lives converted an initial exam to a new start! They are simply handed dental school patients who have already agreed to a procedure. In the real world of dental practice management, new patient success is something every dentist needs to master in order to thrive.

A Treatment Coordination Awakening

I had a treatment coordination awakening that had been brewing for several years. With all the effort that I had put into marketing, patients were coming into my orthodontic practice for exams. But these visits were not converting at an acceptable rate. So, I did the next logical thing. I put a lot of time and resources into developing my treatment coordinator. We hired a sales consultant to visit, record, and coach. We hired experts to teach the verbiage and handling of insurance benefits. We did remote phone training in computer systems and audits of processes. Then I hired a leadership coach. After I spent more than $27,000 in a development effort, my treatment coordinator quit. It was then that I realized what had been missing in our treatment coordination process: taking action.

Taking action comes in many forms. It starts with a sense of urgency by the entire team to start the new patient today. It extends to the patient experience of customer service. It is heavily dependent on follow-up methods, work, and time. It ends with a patient referring another new patient.

The theme of this book is taking action. Treatment coordination is an activity in which every office member participates, especially the doctor. The goal of new patient success is something that must be understood by everyone. It cannot be left to one team member alone, the magical "treatment coordinator," or chance.

Treatment coordination can be quantified. When it comes to patient starts, don't dance around the truth or live in denial of the numbers. Know your statistics. Share your new patient conversion rates at each team meeting. New starts are the lifeblood of your practice, especially if you are a dental specialist. The results reflected in these vital statistics are the responsibility of everyone working in the practice.

I rethought the treatment coordinator process and my new system worked. I realized that focusing on new patient success is something each of us can and must do for a thriving practice. Everyone needs to understand these vital concepts. All need to buy in.

Too many dentists, I believe, live either in servitude or blindness when it comes to the treatment coordination process. My advice is, "Doctors, take control!" It's your business! If your practice is not where you'd like it to be, your new patient conversion rate may be the problem. Fix it!

Once these skills are acquired, education, organization, and implementation of treatment coordination systems can be undertaken. This requires time, attention, and a team devoted to working together to produce immediate results. Efficiency of systems is the end that we wish to achieve, day after day, year after year. This book will describe the means to this end.

Dentistry is, after all, a business. We, as dental professionals, should never lose sight of the fact that we are focused on patients starting and completing their treatment. We must be paid for our services and be profitable. We need to make sales. That's right, sales. As in all businesses, treatment coordination is a sales process. Patients need to say "Yes!" to treatment. To accomplish this, we need to hone our skills of getting to "Yes."

That said, treatment coordination is not just about making the sale. It's also about completing the care plan, having a happy patient, and at the end of it all, making a profit and getting referrals. Once these things are achieved, you've got it made. We want to get treatment coordination right the first time, with every patient. Included in this book are many tips to ensure new patient success. I hope you will enjoy the ideas and discussion. Here's to your treatment coordination success. Now, let's get started.

HOW TO USE THIS BOOK

Let systems run the business
and people run the systems.
People come and go
but systems remain constant.
—Michael E. Gerber

Treatment coordination is a combination of actions put together to get the patient started with dental care. It then includes financial processes and delivery of services. In the end, your patient will be well served, delighted with your excellent treatment, and eager to refer other patients.

Treatment Coordination activities can be divided into three main categories:

   I.   ENGAGEMENT: Welcoming a new patient
  II.   CONVERSION: Starting new treatment
 III. DELIVERY: Gaining patient referrals

All of these processes need to run seamlessly, like a well-oiled machine. This book outlines strategies to conduct a successful new patient exam and experience, negotiate the start of the contract and treatment , deliver dental care seamlessly, and have happy patients who refer their family and friends. Treatment coordination tips will be presented. Use these tactics to fill in your own "to do" list of action items. A sample template is included at the end of this book, as well as a blank one that you can fill in and share with your team.

Part One

ENGAGEMENT

The purpose of business
is to create and keep a customer.
—Peter Drucker

People are brought together: doctor, dental team, and patients. The new patient may have been referred by word-of-mouth from other patients, family, friends, dental colleagues, or another healthcare provider. Or, new patients may be a self-referral after seeing educational material about your practice in the community or on the internet. One thing is consistent: you get one chance to make a good first impression.

Engagement starts with the new patient contacting your office. It starts before the new patient contacts your office with your prospecting outreach in the community, which involves reaching out and welcoming the prospective patient. Your marketing efforts need to be turned into an effective and effusive initial welcome. Now is your chance to engage, delight, and convert a total stranger into a new patient, friend, and referral machine. Now the professionalism, advocacy, and soft skills of the doctor and the customer service team come into play to influence your potential customer to "buy into" your dental services.

Treatment coordination, starting with engagement, is a sales process. All initial clients enter your office seeking your services. Your job is to identify that person's wants and needs, find solutions to their dental health concerns, convince them that you can provide the quality they deserve, and help them get to "Yes" to start their dental treatment. Treatment coordination is a patient journey that you will be taking together. It is time to prepare, take action, and get started.

Chapter 1

PROSPECTING

Most salespeople think that
selling is "closing."
It isn't.
Selling is opening.
—Michael E. Gerber

Each day we have golden moments of opportunity to turn strangers into friends, and visitors into patients. Prospecting in treatment coordination consists of everything that occurs before you get to the patient saying "Yes!" to starting treatment. Prospecting is your preparedness to take every possibility to complete initial exams and get treatment started by taking records. Believing in these opportunities will make you see these opportunities. Believing is seeing.

The word "prospects" has long been used in sales. It denotes the genesis of the sales process. In dentistry, our prospects are future new patients. Just using the term "our future patients" assumes a closing attitude, one of enthusiasm and possibility. Think about potential new patients every day, with every new person you meet. Be confident in your ability to identify and meet your new patients' needs, take great care of them, and become their dentist for a lifetime.

Prospecting can be fun! Today you're hosting an initial exam party and everyone is invited. It's like a first date! Be prepared. It could be love at first sight.

3

Initial Contact

You must understand that seeing is believing,
but also know that believing is seeing.
—Denis Waitley

I have used the phrase "Have you ever considered orthodontic treatment?" thousands of times in my career. We meet people every day who make their way to our dental practices seeking our services. We are the biggest promoters of our own services. We must offer these enthusiastically. We wish that everyone in the world could have access to the excellent dental care that we provide.

There is a need for your services all around you, like gold in the Northern California foothills waiting to be discovered. Are you going to pick up the nuggets? Or are you going to let someone else mine them? New patients are the prospector's gold of your dental practice. These clients are in need of your services. When they understand the value of what you provide, they will start treatment. They will pay for the value that you deliver. Then, once they are fulfilled, they will refer more business to your dental practice.

How do these new patients get established in your dental office in the first place? Treatment coordination begins at the point of entry. Let's examine the possibilities.

Points of Entry
New patients either:

1. Phone the office
2. Email or text the office
3. Walk into the office
4. Arrive via referral from another dentist

Your front desk team must be adept at all of these methods of entry. Here is the start of your potential client conversion funnel. You, your employees, and your systems need to direct each of these entries toward the scheduling of the new patient exam.

1. ANSWERING THE TELEPHONE

Never underestimate the value of your frontline receptionist. New patient calls are the lifeblood of your dental practice. Your patient coordinator controls the success rate of your initial touchpoint: answering the call. Without a successful first phone contact, converting a caller into a patient exam is hard—if not impossible—to achieve.

How are you going to know that the person answering the phone is answering within three rings and doing so "politely?" **Call your own phone.**

Each morning on my drive into my office, I call my office number. This checks that the phone system is working. Increasingly, landlines are being switched to internet service for enhanced reliability. Since changing to internet Weave service, I am happy to report that we have never again had a problem with our lines being down. This was not always the case with previous providers.

Next, I note whether the call is picked up within three rings. I check that the respondent is pleasant, states their name, and is polite. If I can say, "Yes" to all of these things, I know for certain that my phone is answered well. You can also listen to recorded calls, review verbiage, and track results.

A) THE INITIAL PHONE CALL

Be happy in anticipation
of what's coming.
—Abraham Hicks

The phone rings. It's a new patient call. The Eagle has landed. Your mission: make the exam appointment.

1. Get the caller's phone number.
2. Get the caller's name.
3. Make the exam appointment.

Everything after this is icing on the cake. Spend the rest of your time building rapport. Learn more about the new patient and their family and make a connection. Celebrate your new friend.

4. Ask if any other family members need treatment.;
5. Ask about insurance, if applicable.

6. End by confirming the appointment date and time one last time.

Keep it simple. Exam appointment made. Mission accomplished!

Most will agree, it is best to capture the patient's phone number first, just in case the call gets cut off. Your initial focus is scheduling the appointment. Success happens when your three top priorities of the initial phone call are met. Next come numbers four, five, and six.

When you achieve these six things—number, name, appointment, other family members needing treatment, insurance, and confirmation—additional relationship building is at your leisure. Relax and enjoy the rest of the conversation. But, if you don't meet your main objective during the first phone call, you are not helping to make your practice successful.

Your office depends on phone success. If your receptionist is not adept at booking new exams for your practice, you have a problem. If your team spends five minutes chit-chatting on the phone and at the end of it all the initial exam appointment is not made, you need to devote time to retraining.

Once the new patient has been referred or exposed to educational materials about your office, they usually call. This is the chance for your team member to get the job done while portraying your office in the best light possible. The focus and verbal skills of your team on the telephone are reflected in your Key Performance Indicator (KPI): calls converted into exams scheduled.

You can record and review these initial telephone conversations legally, depending upon the laws in your state. Only patients and voice recording can tell you about missed calls. Otherwise, you just don't know. Hopefully, you don't hear about missed calls from patients. Call tracking—twenty-first-century technology—makes the new patient call high priority. You want to answer 100% of new patient calls in an effective manner. The patient called because they are genuinely interested in the treatment offered. It shouldn't be hard to schedule the exam appointment.

Dr. Christopher Phelps is creator of the Call Tracker ROI platform, which offers live listeners, a missed-call dual text alert, and HIPAA-compliant MedChat for messaging. Call Tracker can be linked to your marketing campaigns to record as ROI results. This system can help you close the missed-call loop in your practice.

Other services which offer a variety of instruction for the new patient call include Jay Geier and The Scheduling Institute. Laura Hatch, Front Office Rocks is another. You could try All-Star Dental Academy for additional educational materials. Jayne Bandy of Phone Excellence Mastery provides front-office coaching from Australia. All of these excellent resources provide help with the initial phone call process.

B) PHONE CALL EXAM CONVERSION AND NO-SHOWS

You can be charming on the phone, but never forget that as a front-line receptionist, your job is to get prospective new patients to come into the office for their initial exam. Document all calls requesting an exam. This might be tracked by new names being entered into the computer system. These data need to be recorded. The ratio of initial phone calls to exams scheduled indicates your phone call success rate. Calls not resulting in an appointment being scheduled need follow-up.

New patient exam appointments scheduled but not kept is another important KPI. Your front desk patient coordinator's mission is to schedule exams and fill the treatment schedule. Look at the Exams per Month report. These are exams completed. Print the New Patient Entry report. The difference between these two numbers gives you an idea of your phone call conversion rate to kept exams. You can also run the Exam Status Without Appointments report. These are your exams which failed to show for the exam and were not rescheduled. Call these missed exam families monthly and a very high percentage of these new patients will immediately reschedule.

Your exam no-show rate may actually be higher if your front desk staff did not even enter the information into the computer at the initial phone call. You may have received even more phone calls that didn't schedule exams that you don't know about. To track total calls, you will need to either record all new patient calls or keep track of initial calls by hand. Armed with statistics, your front-desk receptionist can strive to improve each day, week, and month to maximize the calls to exams conversion rate, with an ultimate goal of 100%.

C) RECORDED CALLS AND CALL TRACKING

There's nothing better than the receptionist being empowered to improve by hearing her own recorded voice. Reviewing recorded calls will improve your receptionist's phone skills, as well as give you the phone numbers and times when important new patient phone calls are being missed. What you hear on recorded calls may surprise you.

It is our goal that each new patient inquiry call be answered promptly by a human being. The attitude must be one of anticipation and welcoming.

The call recording service is extremely valuable as an educational tool for the front desk receptionist. If you and your team are able to listen to recorded calls, you can discuss desired changes, make corrections, review scripts, and make needed changes to fine-tune your initial phone call to exam process. Your success rate can then be determined and improved.

For telephone numbers associated with marketing efforts, there are services that will record your initial exam calls at a reasonable rate. Valpak will record your initial calls for just $25 per month. You will receive recorded calls, the success rate of calls answered, days and times of calls, and phone numbers of calls that went to voicemail.

Your recorded calls may surprise you. You may find that a less-experienced team member has more caller enthusiasm than your fifteen-year career veteran. Less-experienced employees tend to answer with energy and delight. It's a thrill for them to answer the phone! They are eager to serve and sincerely interested in the new patient. They sound "all in." Sometimes veteran team members can sound curt, or blasé. Sometimes they may even sound worn out, like they've done this 10,000 times. This is not the initial welcome I want for a new patient. Hear it for yourself to make the office changes you need to make for the best customer service and phone conversion success rate possible.

D) Initial Phone Call Scripting

> *More than 95% of dental offices*
> *do not charge for the initial exam.*
> —Gavriel Asulin

Well-rehearsed scripts are beneficial for uniformity of customer service. Once created, your team needs to internalize these polite and effective words. Your receptionist can add character, humor and their unique personality to get the call job done.

Your receptionist will be asked many questions, including how much the desired treatment costs. Do not refuse this legitimate request. Give a broad range. For example:

> Mrs. Garcia, braces cost between $2,000 and $7,000 dollars depending on the type of treatment, complexity of the case, and length of care. I'd be happy to set up a complimentary exam

appointment with Dr. Gorczyca, who is a board-certified ortho-dontist with thirty years' experience, to review your personalized treatment plan and financial estimate for the care you need.

It is best for your team member not to enter information into the computer system as she gathers the patient information and carries on the new patient conversation. Doing so risks slowing speech and sounding like an automaton. Be fully engaged. Basic information can be handwritten on an intake sheet and later transferred electronically. Remember to have the patient's preferred language also recorded. That way, if it becomes necessary to respond to further questions in the future, your Spanish-speaking receptionist, for example, can be the one to answer the questions. Create a system to be able to print out reports of Spanish speakers for this purpose.

You may want to ask your new patient, "What do you know about the orthodontic treatment you need?" In this way, you may find out if you are a second opinion. You may also want to ask, "What do you know about our office?" or "How were you referred?" If you are a second opinion, consider: "Mrs. Garcia, you are heading toward a big decision; I suggest that you come in for a second opinion. When can you come in for a complimentary exam, morning or afternoon?" After this exam, you want to be their top choice and final opinion.

E) BUSIEST TIMES OF NEW PATIENT CALLS

Productivity is never an accident.
It is always the result of a commitment to excellence,
intelligent planning, and focused effort.
—Paul J. Meyer

At Gorczyca Orthodontics in Antioch, California, the results of our recording system indicate that the two busiest times for calls to our practice are on Tuesdays from 8:00 to 9:00 a.m. and from 12:00 to 2:00 p.m. Orthodontist Jamie Reynolds of Detroit, Michigan, reports that his peak business times are Fridays from 12:00 p.m. to 2:00 p.m. These data indicate that **it is essential that your phone be answered during the lunch hour by a human being** for the greatest success scheduling new exams. Cross-train additional team members and have receptionists stagger lunch breaks to get this job done. If you are short-staffed or you find that your only receptionist is without a back-up during lunch, you may choose to add a local or national service such as Dental Support Specialties of Ohio (www.DentalSupportSpecialties. com) to handle your lunch-time calls.

F) Do Not Interrupt the Initial Phone Call

I was once banned from walking behind the receptionist's desk during patient hours. Why? Because doctors interrupt receptionists during new patient calls! This is a critical time when all attention needs to be placed on the new patient.

Create a silent signal in your dental office or a rule so that initial patient calls are not interrupted. Your receptionist may want to lift a finger to their lips as in the universal, "Quiet, please" sign. You may even want to direct new patient calls to a back line, away from others. Whatever you do, give your new patient call the importance and attention that it deserves.

G) Call Entries

The number of new calls resulting in new exams should appear on your day sheet. This information needs to be reviewed in order to assess how many new exams were scheduled that day. Have your receptionist report the call numbers at your weekly or monthly team meeting. This phone-answering skill accountability will give your frontline receptionist a goal and a sense of achievement. It will also give you the first critical number of your treatment coordination funnel: new patient calls.

Make note of how the patient was referred. Assigning different numbers to marketing campaigns and mailings will simplify tracking. In this way, your internal, external, and relationship referral marketing can be evaluated on a regular basis.

1. E-mails to the Office

Is there more you could do to direct new patients to your website? How many contacts are you getting per month from your webpage? Do you include your URL on all printed and digital media as well as on your electronic signature? A simple "Visit Us at (your URL)" can help. Since you are checking e-mails received via your web portal daily, run the website report as well.

2. WALK-INS

Each day we have the opportunity to make new contacts in our office. They come from all parts of our community—vendors, passersby, patients' family members or friends, and new referrals from other doctors. Walk-ins are a big new patient opportunity. Think of all office walk-ins as new friends and potential new patients.

A) PEOPLE WE MEET IN THE COMMUNITY

Be prepared at all times to invite new acquaintances to your office. Staff wearing shirts and jackets with your logo out in the community can help. Having business cards handy facilitates follow-through. Having a prepared "elevator pitch" of what to say makes the process even easier. When asked, "Tell me about your office," what do you say? At Gorczyca Orthodontics, we reply: "We are clinically excellent, we offer great customer service, and it would be a great patient experience for you and your family to receive your treatment at our office. We will take great care of you." These are our three core values, known by all. We walk this talk each day at Gorczyca Orthodontics along with the vision that, "smiles change lives."

B) VISITORS

Visitors include everyone from delivery persons to those asking for directions as well as patients' family and friends. Welcome them as prospective patients and you may soon see them in your dental chair.

I remember doing orthodontic treatment on the son of our mail carrier. One day she asked if we did braces, and then brought her son in for an orthodontic exam and subsequent treatment. Another time someone came to our office by mistake. They had scheduled an initial orthodontic exam in another office. They then stayed and completed their exam and started treatment in our office. Wrong office, right patient! We couldn't believe it!

Never miss an opportunity to schedule an initial exam. Next time you have a visitor to your office try the magic words, "While you're here, would you like to schedule or do a new patient exam?"

C) PASSERSBY

Exclusive shopping centers such as Broadway Plaza in Walnut Creek, California, put stand-up signs out on the sidewalk each day. They are eye-catching and highlight the products on offer. They tend to add a colorful dog bowl or balloons. It's cute, branded marketing. Whether you are in a professional building, mall, or office complex, many people pass your dental practice on a daily basis. Catch their attention with an informative sign.

Dental coach Mark Rossi of Minnesota, in a podcast with Dr. Howard Farran, stated that the first thing that he does when he advises a new dental office is to give high priority to the signage. Mr. Rossi claims the addition of a sign can improve initial exams by as much as 50%. Try, "We Welcome All Smiles" with your office name as a start.

d) Family of Patients

Your reception areas are filled each day with additional family members who need your dental services. Invite relatives to schedule a visit for themselves. Make it a habit to ask, "Is there anyone else in the family who may be in need of our dental care?" Be sure to ask this question during the initial exam process and during check-out.

You may want to start a club for younger children. We offer "Club Braces." Keep the office fun. Give prizes. Little kids love pretend rings, toys, stuffed animals, and super balls. Feature a treasure chest. You may want to have an adult treasure chest of oral hygiene products. Your office should be a giving place where everyone in the family can look forward to visiting and having their dental treatment.

Do what the great bookstores and car dealerships do. Provide refreshments. Have hot chocolate, coffee and tea available with a Keurig machine. Add water bottles with branded, custom labels. Cookies and healthy treats can also be served. Encourage your patient families to stick around, and personally take the opportunity to walk out into the reception area to welcome them. While you're there, try the "whalya" approach of dentist Dr. Tom Orent. Try asking, "Whalya here, would you like an initial exam?"

e) Friends of Patients

Consider friends of your patients as "window shoppers." In orthodontics, it is not unusual to have a reception room full of friends. At Gorczyca Orthodontics, we offer seats by the treatment chairs where friends can sit during the orthodontic appointment. High school students often bring their boyfriend or girlfriend to the appointment. In this way, we get to know quite a number of new people each day. Let them know that your office has complimentary initial exams, and hand them a "Refer a Friend" gift card.

F) GRANDPARENTS OF PATIENTS

It's never too late for a beautiful smile. If you are treating many children and teens in your dental practice, you may want to create a special invitation for grandparents, who often drive children to their dental appointments. The same is true for nannies. Ask them to become your patient. If you are a pediatric dentist, ask the grandparents if they need a dentist, and then provide a referral to a dental colleague.

3. DOCTOR REFERRALS

Create a list of all dentists in your area. Then call them personally. Take time to get to know them. You are part of a larger dental community. Doctor referrals are part of our good treatment. Once this is done, work toward making appropriate referrals which you will receive in return. Even if you are a general dentist, you have the opportunity to gain many patients from your specialist colleagues.

There are several ways that doctor referrals come to your dental office: by snail mail, telephone, fax, e-mail, web portal, text, or in person. You may have received a prepaid postage card which you had given in triplicate pad form to all of your referring offices. Once you receive this card, call the patient. Keep trying to contact them until an appointment is scheduled. If you have no response within thirty days, despite at least three calls, e-mails, or texts, let the referring office know. This is especially important with periodontal disease and pathology patients who are in urgent need of an evaluation. Send the referring doctor a letter informing them that the patient is being negligent in their own health and never showed up. You need this documentation of all calls and attempts to schedule. Do everything you can to help patients receive the care that they need.

The new patient may walk in to make their exam appointment. Many patients come directly from their previous dental appointment. Patients may call from the referring doctor's office. Always ask the patient how they were referred so that you can thank the appropriate doctor and send exam reports.

Referral Thank You

We must stop and thank
the people who make a difference in our lives.
—John F. Kennedy

The most effective way to compliment those who refer new patients is to pick up the phone and thank them personally. You may also want to send a thank-you card once the patient has started treatment. Even a small gift in friendship is appreciated from time to time.

I love delivering edible goodies to those offices that have provided excellent, collegial care. In the state of California, according to the California Dental Board, gifts can be given as a token of friendship but not in direct response to patient referrals. Let your colleagues, patients, and team members know how much you appreciate them and referrals will take care of themselves.

Chapter 2

THE TEAM

*Great vision without great people
is irrelevant.*
—Jim Collins

No one can efficiently and effectively run all of the treatment coordination processes alone. As the doctor, other than performing the exam, diagnosis, and designing the plan for the new patient, you will need help from your capable team members every step of the way.

Treatment coordination can be divided into three major work functions: sales/marketing, service operations, and financial systems. The team working in synergy drives the treatment coordination engine.

THE DREAM TEAM

Jim Collins, author of *Good to Great* describes the ideal team as "having the right people in the right seats on the bus." Finding someone loyal to your practice, doing what you have hired them to do, and producing the results you want, is not easy. You and your "dream team" produce new patient conversion results. The doctor and team gain case acceptance, deliver the treatment, and collect the payment. Jeff Palmer of Case Conversion Institute calls this "Say, Do, Pay." Simply stated, it consists of diagnosis and treatment plan, service, and payment.

SERVICE OPERATIONS

Gino Wickman's book, *Get a Grip,* outlines the staff evaluation process as having three critical components: the person who "gets it," "wants it," and is "capable to do it." He abbreviates this process as GWC. I think of these three essentials as being "ready, willing, and able." To have all three of these qualities together in a loyal employee is essential for top performance.

JOB DESCRIPTIONS

> *Delegation is not like putting your kid up for adoption.*
> *Delegation is like hiring a babysitter.*
> —Bruce Tulgan

In order to have workplace requirements clearly understood, job descriptions are paramount. If more than one person is responsible for a task, no one is responsible. These can be reviewed individually with each team member and collectively at your staff meetings. Tasks are assigned specifically to individuals. Leave nothing to chance.

KPIs (Key Performance Indicators), are numbers to shoot for, outcome goals. For example, making forty new patient follow-up phone calls per day might be one KPI given to a treatment coordinator. Scheduling forty-two new patient exams per month could be another. Starting twenty-five new patients per month could be a third.

Setting KPIs gives everyone on the team an understanding of what work needs to be done and what success looks like. As the doctor/owner of your dental practice, you may think that job activities are self-evident. I assure you; they are not. Never assume that anyone on the team will do anything unless asked to do so. Even putting the mail in the mailbox needs to be someone's designated task.

I remember once asking, "Who is responsible for managing the doctor-patient referral cards that we receive in the mail?" I patiently waited for a response from my team. No one replied. Although I had three front-desk receptionists at the time, no one took it upon herself to call new patients. Neither did the treatment coordinator. I was shocked! Needless to say, this task was immediately given to the receptionist seated closest to the door. The additional responsibility of a "Welcome Concierge" was created.

Assigning individual tasks is not micro-management. From time to time, you will get pushback and be told, "Don't micromanage me!" Checking that your office systems are running like a well-oiled machine is not looking over someone's shoulder! It is doing your job responsibly; this is your duty as a practice owner or manager. Once you have verified that tasks are being completed, you will have confidence that you can count on performance. You then have the right people in the right seats on your bus.

High-performing team members will present their results voluntarily; they will complete their duties and produce at a level higher than you requested or even expected. Treat these employees like gold. They make every day in your dental practice a joy.

All duties also need to be carried through to completion. When you cannot find someone to do a particular job that needs to be done, then you as the business leader will be reassigning it, doing it yourself, or hiring someone new to do it. As the practice owner, you need to hear "Yes!" from each team member in the form of performance and the results that you seek. If the employee is not fully ready, willing, and able, and if the team does not trust that an individual has these three characteristics for the job that needs to be done, then you need to make a change.

If you know someone cannot do a task well, it will take courage, candor, and communication to recognize this deficiency and act, for the greater good of the organization. This may not be the right job for that person. If you have open-book meetings and report key metrics, lack of performance will become evident. No one wants to let the team down. Eventually, the underachiever—someone incompetent or unwilling to carry their weight—will resign. This result is much better than maintaining someone who is always "dropping the ball."

Real-time performance appraisals, especially when things are not going well, are one of the hardest aspects of dental office management. If you don't address the problem—i.e., identify, discuss, and solve the issues holding performance back on a regular basis—disappointment and irritation will fester and grow. You will be stuck at the mercy of the weakest link. So be strong, vigilant, and proactive in order to restore and maintain your office performance, leadership, and success.

What Makes a Great Treatment Coordinator?

Maybe you're thinking that you want to hire a treatment coordinator (TC), that one special person with drive and talent who will help you complete the exam, review financial arrangements, and start the treatment process. By following up with exam patients who do not sign up the day of the exam, your TC team member can help to build your practice. Should this important role be assigned, your TC's talent and performance are critical to the success of your practice. What skills and characteristics will you look for when hiring this key individual? Here are a few attributes that make this key player more likely to succeed.

1. Tenacious

The treatment coordinator must **never give up.** He or she must be conscientious and determined in the goal of scheduling. You cannot assign this most important job to someone with poor attendance or few working hours. **Treatment coordination is a five-days-a-week full time job.** Together with the financial coordinator, the treatment coordinator needs to be highly available and reliable.

Part of the tenacity of sales is knowing that daily follow-up needs to be tackled with urgency, sustained effort, and determination. There needs to be laser focus on the task of scheduling and confirming new patient exams, assisting the doctor with the exam, answering questions, completing insurance preauthorization, and ultimately starting treatment. Help can be provided by the front desk staff, but ultimately, one person needs to responsible for exam conversion success.

2. Organized

Following up with several patients per day will require a methodical and organized approach. Patient information must be entered into HIPAA-compliant electronic databases. To optimize scheduling, reports of patients needing callbacks will be regularly reviewed. Practice management reports include: referrals, exams missed, exams completed, and follow-up exams. Additional patient questions need to be handled on a daily basis. Pending-exam phone calls need to be made each day. The will-call list of patients who have procrastinated and not yet started treatment needs to be constantly addressed. All of these tasks take time and focus but remain a top priority in your treatment coordination office schedule.

3. Empathetic

> *Empathy is about standing in someone else's shoes,*
> *feeling with his or her heart, seeing with his or her eyes.*
> —Daniel H. Pink

The TC must be a warm and empathetic communicator who is able to understand and work with the patient's needs and family situation. This person must love people. The TC needs to be knowledgeable and enthusiastic about dental products and services, and must feel the role as a calling to help patients receive the dental care they need and deserve. It should be the TC's vision that "Smiles change lives," and that the work is making a difference in patient's lives.

4. Resourceful

The TC must be able to read the patient and make the payment plans work for them. The person in this role is a problem solver, and needs to be able to reason well and think quickly. The TC must possess the skills to outline financial contracts, verify insurance, and facilitate the use of third-party lending agencies. The TC needs to get the payment plan solidified at the time of the initial exam so the patient can start treatment.

5. Thick-Skinned

The TC can't take negative responses personally. A yes or no answer is perfectly acceptable. It's the "I need to think about it," or "I need to talk to someone," or "I don't know" answers that are the true rejections which need to be minimized. The TC needs to keep the conversation moving forward, continuing to ask questions, building a relationship, and serving the patient—striving always to generate a "Yes!" to starting treatment.

6. A Winner's Mentality

> *Ability is what you're capable of doing.*
> *Motivation determines what you do.*
> *Attitude determines how well you do it.*
> —Lou Holtz

The TC must have a winner's instinct, drive, and motivation, as well as confidence and high self-esteem. To be successful, TCs must *want* to win, make the sale, and help the patient. This is the most important characteristic of all.

Some call this the "killer instinct." I call it the "winner's instinct" —a competitive advantage. It is an unstoppable force that characterizes a high-achievement personality—not easily derailed by daily urgencies, side-tracking attention grabbers, or disturbances. This is a personality of grit and persistence.

MEETING PULSE

*Unbridled enthusiasm is
the raw motiving power of teams.*
—Katzenbach & Smith

Short term outcomes affect everyone's paycheck. If metrics are regularly reviewed in real time, there are no surprises at performance reviews, bonus or salary reviews, or end of the year summaries. On a weekly basis, each team member can report his or her progress toward the treatment coordination numbers via their individual KPIs. Metrics can include exams scheduled; exams completed; records scheduled; starts completed; follow-up phone calls made; and referrals from doctors, patients, the internet, or the community. This is your team score. This way, everyone is on board and excited about their daily progress.

Tony Hsieh, CEO of Zappos, is famous for paying employees $2,000 to leave. This is his strategy to get non-performing staff to quit. It may be unrealistic to pay $2,000 for an unengaged dental staff person to leave your practice. You could, however, get the same result by simply saying, "If you don't think you want to work here, I would prefer that you go."

If you question whether someone wants office success, pay attention to talk of quitting. Chances are such chatter will translate into leaving soon. In fact, if you hear someone question whether they will stay at your dental office, you might as well ask them for their resignation in writing, right then and there. This person lacks drive and enthusiasm and is certainly not "all in." See what happens. Either the employee with shape up or ship out.

The Peter Principle

*In a hierarchy, every employee tends to rise
to his level of incompetence.*
—Laurence J. Peter and Raymond Hull

Jolene has been doing an excellent job as clinical director at Gorczyca Orthodontics for more than twenty-two years. Each time the office opportunity for promotion came, Jolene declined. Jolene loves her clinical orthodontic patients and prefers not to spend time at the front desk. Before working at Gorczyca Orthodontics, Jolene worked in a clinic with pediatric dentistry patients. She has continued to do her job as a clinical registered dental assistant (RDA) flawlessly for over thirty-eight years. She never changed positions. She just kept doing the job she loved as a dental assistant, with excellence.

Often in dentistry, we make the mistake of promoting experienced team members to new roles as treatment coordinators or office managers based on tenure rather than passion or skill set. We fail to realize that a dental front office position as treatment coordinator, financial coordinator, or office manager requires completely different personality traits and skills as compared to the role of a clinical dental assistant. A chairside assistant works closely with the doctor and with others. The roles of office manager or treatment coordinator require self-direction and independence. These positions require a high level of confidence and assertiveness.

I have started to think more deeply about these talented, long-term employees who become disillusioned in their new higher-level positions as office managers or treatment coordinators. Often a chairside assistant may not perform well in this new position. This is not what we, as business owners, intend. Dentists and owners are also looking for team promotion and development opportunities. Yet, our office experience often validates the Peter Principle. *The Peter Principle,* written by Laurence J. Peter and Raymond Hull, simply states, "In a hierarchy, every employee tends to rise to his level of incompetence."

Why does it happen to us in dentistry? Not promoting a loyal team member creates a difficult hiring dilemma for the dental business owner. The senior employee doesn't want to see a new hire in a position of responsibility and pay perceived as "higher" than their own. They want their commitment to be rewarded. Yet, because of the independence, leadership, and management skills required by the promotion, bringing in a fresh hire might be exactly what needs to be done for the TC or manager success of the practice. An objective job talent search needs to be done.

The Peter Principle is rampant in dentistry. Dental consultant Lisa Mergens states that this is most prevalent in the case of the office "manager" position. Often, a receptionist or assistant who has tenure and no management experience is elevated to this new role. A working interview is not done to evaluate their ability for being an administrator and a liaison for the doctor and no longer simply a member of the team. The employee may rise to the new level of responsibility, but often struggles or fails to perform the full job functions.

Another Peter Principle scenario could go like this: You hire an employee to be a chairside RDA. She is super-competent. You promote her to the position of records coordinator. She is reasonably good. The TC position then opens up. You trust and know this long-term employee. You think it would be wonderful to have the records coordinator do the exam and follow through directly into the records appointment. You believe she can do it, and it satisfies your desire to provide a job development opportunity. You also know that an entry-level person is much easier to find than a more highly-skilled and experienced hire who needs to be familiar with the office management computer software system. So, you automatically promote your dental assistant for this most important management job without posting the job opening to find the most qualified and talented candidate. You then hire a new entry level person to fill the former position.

You then spend tens of thousands of dollars training your employee in her new sales role as treatment coordinator. You want this individual to do well, but training doesn't work. A clear job description and the assigned KPIs don't register. **Treatment coordination is sales,** but this person does not have the instinct to take action and follow-up to start new cases. She may not even like this new role. She wanted the promotion, the higher salary, and the private office. Once received, she realizes she doesn't want to be alone in the TC room. So, she spends most of her time talking at the front desk.

If you believe you're getting a "C" performance, you must do something about it! Make a change to bring performance back up to an "A" grade. It won't be easy. Feathers will be ruffled. There will be pushback. You may even see the sign of a truly bad attitude: the infamous eye roll. But, as difficult as the process is, you can improve and eliminate poor performance and behaviors forever. Don't run away from the obvious. Take action!

Responsibility

> *Trust is the great simplifier.*
> *If people in business told the truth,*
> *80 to 90 percent of their problems would disappear.*
> —William Schutz

Follow-up phone calls, emails, and text messaging are the bottleneck of treatment coordination. The follow-up process takes discipline. However, with tenacity to the point of routine, I suggest that calls, emails, texts, and sending postcards can actually be enjoyable. In order to not become tedious, these activities need to be divided amongst everyone on the team of a thriving dental practice. The individual tasks can be rotated. The majority of this book is about constant communication until a response is generated. I would like to talk more about these techniques, but first I want to give you something interesting to think about.

Faced with these tasks, you might hear your team member say, "I don't have time." Ask "What are you spending your time doing?" You might hear, "I'm busy." Ask: "Busy doing what? What could be more important than making calls or following-up with potential new patients?"

Nothing builds a practice faster than new patient phone calls. It's good customer service and the foundation of the treatment coordination process. Start by printing up your new patient Pending List. How many names are on the list? Equally divide the list between all able callers in your office. Have each person complete the calls. Ask each one how many new patient appointments they scheduled. This will give you an understanding of the completion of this all-important task in your office and who would be best to do it.

Now if someone on your team is not making calls or getting other assignments done, what might they be doing? These two classic time-wasters rang true to me, so I need to take a moment to share them with you and review their symptoms.

1. Papyromania

The papyromaniac will have a messy desk, with disorganized piles of papers. Stacks of letters, bills, and patient data to be filed are used as an excuse to mask the inability to do real work. When approached, they will give the illusion that there is too much work to be done. Just look at their desk! How could they possibly do one thing more? In reality, due to lack of organization, the papyromaniac is doing very little. The papyromaniac hides behind a cluttered in-basket which never moves to the out-basket.

2. Papyrophobia

Equally dangerous is the papyrophobe who obsessively maintains a completely clean but totally unproductive desk! Here, desk cleaning to the point of compulsion takes priority over attending to new patients. In the worst-case scenario, they cannot tolerate papers anywhere in the office. Vital papers, such as dental license renewals, bills, or important patient communications can be thrown away in the desk cleaning purge!

Doctor, the Problem is You!

> *"Temet Nosce"*
> *Know thyself.*
> —Gary Vaynerchuk

I once heard a speaker quote the great business manager, J. W. "Bill" Marriott, who said, "If you have a fly in your kitchen, you opened the window!" What you tolerate, occurs. So what is the most likely diagnosis of your team problems? You!

What are you blind to? An outside coach will be able to detect employee problems with an objective eye long before you, as the doctor, will. Having close relationships with your team members could lead to performance issues being overlooked. Whatever happens in your dental practice, you, as the doctor/owner, are responsible. Once you accept this fact, life will become easier. You can make the changes that you need to improve.

Start by making a "great employees only" rule. Focus on acquisition, development, and retention of talent. Eliminate staff who do not show up, show up late, drop the ball, make excessive mistakes and excuses, and cause you grief. Your future self, team, and patients will thank you for it!

Now I know what you're thinking. It's human nature to "pass the buck" and play the blame game. There is no blaming others. If change is needed, it's up to you to *take action* and get it done. You and everyone on your team are the active contributors. Adopt the "if it is to be, it's up to me" mentality.

If I See It, I Own It

When you have a start lead, there should be absolutely no confusion that the person who gets the lead should make the records appointment right then and there. Cross-training is key. You don't want opportunity to pass because not everyone on the team is capable of starting a new patient in the office.

Same-day starts give you a 100% conversion rate for that patient. Do it often enough, and you may have a 100% conversion rate for that day. Always offer to complete records at the time of the initial exam when the treatment is first recommended. Stay late, work through lunch, or change the schedule. Get the job done with a great deal of satisfaction that you are moving closer to your success goal.

The patient came in wanting treatment. Give it to them. There is no need to delay, no passing the buck to the next person, procrastinating to a day later, a week later, or next month. Tomorrow often never comes. Next month starts a new cycle. Lack of confidence in the process of starting a new patient and taking initial records today should not be a problem for anyone in the office. If you already take an initial panorex and photos during your initial exam process, finishing records and starting treatment is a breeze!

Outside Jobs

Outside jobs may affect individual and team performance. They might become a conflict of interest. Watch out for the individual doing something other than that for which you are paying. Left unattended, a college student hired to answer phones in the afternoon may be doing schoolwork instead of focusing on incoming calls. A side business could be selling weight-loss products or being an Avon Lady. With conflicting activities, your employee is not fully focused on your patients and your business while at work.

A Bonus System

When there is no guessing to your start goal for the month, you may want to attach this outcome to a bonus program. In his book, *The Scheduling Institute*, consultant Jay Geier recommends rewards be based upon the number of new case starts. Figure out your bare assessment minimum (BAM) number as the basis for your incentive system. In our orthodontic office, our bonus is $180 for eighteen orthodontic case starts and increases $10 up to twenty-one cases. At twenty-two cases, it goes to $250. At twenty-three cases, it goes to $500. At twenty-four cases, it goes to $750, and at twenty-five cases it goes to $1,000. What's important is the summit of a $1,000 bonus per team member. That is what catches attention and inspires people to work a little bit harder. When you reach your amazing goal, celebrate!

Although there are other profit incentives such as 401(k) profit-sharing retirement plan contributions, most team members do not value this benefit as much as seeing a monetary reward going directly into their checking account. A bonus system allows your office to hold base salaries at a level that gives job security while sharing the success that comes with increasing numbers of new patients, production, and collections. The more generated, the more earned. This usually sounds good to everyone.

Chapter 3

SOFT SKILLS

Charisma is the transference
of enthusiasm.
—Ralph Archbold

It's energizing and empowering. It demonstrates personal excitement, confidence, and success. It expresses high expectations and engages people. What is it? It is charisma. And, if you've got it, you are going to be great at treatment coordination.

Charisma makes someone immediately feel that they like you. The science of charisma can be broken down to subtle acts that we can all work on. We can affect what a patient may do if we appeal to their emotions. Knowing and applying these small traits of charisma to any person in sales is beneficial, especially in the dental office.

Purchases are made using emotion, not logic. How you present yourself and the culture of your office play a big role in your patient feeling comfortable, having trust in your care, and saying "yes" to treatment.

WELCOME REMINDER CALL

Imagine that you make an appointment with a new doctor three months in advance. But then your child has a school play on the same day. With your focus on this family event, you miss your dental appointment. You forget. It happens to everyone.

Call your patient, two days before the initial exam appointment. Don't rely solely on electronic messaging or voice-recorded reminders. Your personal welcome reminder call will be your initial contact and your first impression. Here you not only remind the family of their initial visit, but you are also starting your new patient relationship. The quality of the call elevates you one more step above expectations.

A WARM WELCOME

Imagine your best friend from high school coming to your home as a guest. How would you personally answer the door? Would you stand to greet them with a warm smile and touch? Would you say: "Hello, come in. We're so happy to see you. How are you today? Please make yourself comfortable. Is there anything we can get you?"

Lights on, doors unlocked. Our uniforms look sharp and there's a smile on our faces. We're ready and prepared to meet the first new patient of the day. The office concierge or greeter seated closest to the door is ready for patients. When the new patient and family members enter, she stands, introduces herself, and extends her hand to shake up and down twice gently (the royal handshake). The patient is offered refreshments and given an office tour.

The new patient and their family will form their first impression within the first seven seconds of entering your office. Whatever job title you want to give it—Greeter, Concierge, or New Patient Experience Coordinator—make warm welcome preparedness part of your daily schedule. Don't leave this important first step to chance.

The front desk concierge is the best person to have a list of the day's new patients printed and posted at her computer terminal so she can welcome them as soon as they arrive. Should a patient be more than seven minutes late, she can call to verify that they are still on their way and help them with directions.

No matter what is going on in your office, **be on time for the initial exam.** If possible, have the front desk concierge bring the family into the exam room ten minutes early. Start early or on time. Once the patient is ultimately escorted to the initial exam area, the patient may already feel that they have made a good choice.

Use the New Patient's Name

> *Names are the sweetest and most important sound*
> *in any language.*
> —Dale Carnegie

"Mr. Bond, Mr. James Bond." "Welcome to our office, James. I'm Lyndsay; I will be helping you today. Thank you for coming in."

Repeat the patient's name as often as possible during the new patient exam process. Placing a sign in the exam room will help the doctor remember the patient's name. This welcome sign can be given to the family placed in their welcome folder after the exam. Patients love this! It shows a personal touch and makes the new patient feels like a VIP.

Be Knowledgeable About the New Patient

As the new patient is guided to the examination chair, now is the time for small talk. Make your guest comfortable and relaxed. Ask questions. Let them tell you about themselves.

What are their hobbies and interests? Are they married? Do they have children? Why are they seeking dental treatment at this time? This information can be obtained verbally and via a questionnaire.

If you have a treatment coordinator, have her spend a few minutes becoming more knowledgeable about the patient. What do they do for a living? What do they want from their dental treatment? Do they have a general dentist? Who was their last dentist? The treatment coordinator can provide a debriefing to the doctor before entering the examination room.

Finally, take time to go over the health history. The doctor must review and sign the health history before beginning the exam.

Smile

> *Every time you smile at someone,*
> *it is an action of love,*
> *a gift to that person,*
> *a beautiful thing.*
> —Mother Teresa

What can we do within the first seven seconds to make ourselves appear attractive, friendly, and charismatic? Smile. A smile is the universal welcome. It will put the new patient at ease. When you meet your new patient, pretend you are meeting a longtime friend. If you smile, the patient will smile back. Suddenly you have a new friend.

PROFESSIONAL DRESS

Patients expect their doctors to be sharp in appearance and knowledge. Dress for success and wear great clothes! If you are a woman, consider wearing heels. If you are a man, consider a tie and a long-sleeve shirt.

In my book, *At Your Service: 5-Star Customer Care for a Successful Dental Practice,* I cite a study where doctor's dress was analyzed through a patient questionnaire. It was determined that patients prefer their doctor to be well dressed and not in scrubs. Always wear professional clothes in the office. If you would like more information about creating a successful professional look, visit Janice Hurley, image expert, at www.janicehurley.com.

POSTURE

Chin up, shoulders back, stand up straight just like your mother told you. Before you enter the exam room, do an arm and shoulder stretch and take a deep breath. Good posture will give you higher energy. Perhaps you have come from the clinical area where you have been hunched over a patient. Take a moment to loosen up. On initial contact, body language is four times more important than what you say to a new patient. Walk into the room tall, then extend your hand to welcome everyone in the room.

BODY LANGUAGE

Before you start your intraoral exam, sit across from your patient. Observe their face and eyes, face-to-face. Lean in slightly as you speak, but don't get too close as to invade their private space. Give them at least two feet. If the patient leans back, you lean back. Lean in together, lean out together. This is the dance of the new exam.

As you speak with your new patient, imagine them saying to you, "Look at my eyes." Notice their eye color. Is it blue, green, or brown? This will reassure that you are looking into their eyes. As you are doing so, you are looking into their thoughts and giving them your full attention. Ask them to tell you what they would like to change about their teeth. Then take time to listen.

Breaking the Ice

If you haven't orchestrated it
you don't own it.
—Michael E. Gerber

Step one of every life relationship: introduce yourself. Make a human connection. A little humor is the best ice breaker. Take advantage of the opportunity to share a laugh or anything else that you have in common with your new patient and their family.

In the exam, the TC and doctor will quickly get to know the new patient and their family. In return, the new patient will be doing the same. Act as if the patient has already made the decision to have treatment done at your office. Relax and enjoy the moment.

Take care not to have interruptions during the sacred exam. Everyone on the team needs to understand that this one transaction, the initial exam, is responsible for the success of the practice and their own personal success. During this time, your attention and focus are solely on the new patient. Everything else can be shut out for a short time. No doors opening, no one saying, "Doctor, you're needed." No interruptions.

If necessary, a light system can signal the doctor that they are wanted in another area of the office, but no sounds need to be heard. Should the exam go on too long, the treatment coordinator can stand and *silently* signal the doctor that is it time to go. A light finger tap on the shoulder also works. Whether you are in an exam room or a clinical area, this method can be politely used.

The Exam

*One of the biggest mistakes dentists and orthodontists make
is that they are too technical when talking to their patients.*
—Ashley Latter

When the patient is done telling you everything that they would like to say, begin your initial exam. Ask them, "What can we do to get you to love your smile?" Then listen. Active listening is essential. Don't interrupt.

Explain that your assistant will be taking notes during the exam. Announce your findings and point them out in addressing the patient's chief complaint. Your treatment coordinator may have already taken a panoramic radiograph and done clinical photos. These can also be used to demonstrate and share your clinical findings with your patient.

Describe the diagnosis and treatment plan in lay terms, and give the patient and their family the assurance that doing business with your office will be enjoyable and easy. Present simply and succinctly. People are busy and have a lot on their minds. Don't overdo the details. Your patient doesn't want to hear about minutiae. Necessary details can be written in the final treatment plan document that will be signed later.

Present your action plan and emphasize that now is the best time to get started. Address the patient's concerns and let them know how you will resolve their biggest perceived problem. Recommend starting treatment soon. End the exam by reassuring the patient that you will take great care of them.

Visual Aids

*People who make the greatest use of
company-supplied visual aids are the top producers.*
—Tom Hopkins

Showing your new patient their own photos and radiographs is extremely powerful. Therefore, schedule enough exam time (one hour if possible) to gather these records in presentation-ready format to use during your new patient exam.

Visual aids allow you to deliver more information in less time. Having your new patient's photos and display books of completed cases similar to the patient's case builds confidence. Have models of the appliances or restorations that you offer and are planning to use. Hand these props to the patient to evaluate. Let them touch the samples, enabling them to actively participate in choosing which variety of treatment they would like.

Let the patient say, "I would like this one." This is music to the doctor and treatment coordinators ears. It's as good as a "yes" to treatment. With this comment, your work may be done. Make note of this choice on the patient's paperwork and move toward scheduling the appointment to start treatment.

The Wow Factor

> *Treat every appointment like an event-*
> *make it special for each patient.*
> —Ashley Latter

Before you end the exam process, ask yourself, does your presentation have a little "Wow"? At Gorczyca Orthodontics, we have successfully treated more than 10,000 patients. Wow! Don't be boring, be memorable!

Think about what you could discuss using the word "Wow!" Describe yourself and your office. Whatever amazing things you can say about your office or the doctor, do it. It could be awards or accolades, the number of patients treated, accomplishments in the community, or things you're doing that no one else can.

Display confidence! Be sincere, positive, focused, polished, and enthusiastic about what special things you have to offer. Be outstandingly memorable.

Interdisciplinary Dental Care

Many dental patients need multiple services and specialists to fulfill their comprehensive treatment plan. Make interdisciplinary care easy. Orthodontists are often the quarterback of this process because we have full records and may make a physical diagnostic wax-up or a virtual setup of anticipated results. The Invisalign ClinCheck® can be used to display virtual results. The physical setups can be held in the hand of the patient. This is powerful and especially helpful in case acceptance of large, full-mouth reconstruction cases.

If you are part of an interdisciplinary team, you can all meet together to outline the patient's treatment plan sequence step by step. Having this outline will make treatment efficient and seamless for everyone involved, including the patient.

THE NEW PATIENT EXAM

I once gave a practice management lecture at a nearby dental school. The topic was customer service. When we got to the part that focused on the new patient experience, I asked the young doctors how they were feeling about their success rate of new patient exam conversions. I asked them how many new patient exams they had done. The answer was "Zero."

These students were about to be launched out into the working world and they had no experience performing the one act that will determine their ultimate success or failure, the initial new patient exam. This is a crucial aspect of treatment coordination, with many roles to be played. I hope that the following descriptions will be of value to all dental graduates, both recent and remote.

EXAM TO RECORDS STATUS

Once the initial exam is completed, patients who scheduled their next appointment will be changed to records status. Patients who have not committed to treatment will now be changed to pending status.

It is unusual for a patient to tell you, "No, I will not be starting treatment in your office" the day of the initial exam. In thirty years of practice, I don't recall a single patient ever telling me this. Most patients are nice people and don't want to openly reject you. If they don't start treatment immediately after the exam, it is normal to hear an excuse.

DIAGNOSIS AND TREATMENT PLAN

In my orthodontic office, we include a line at the bottom of your clinical exam sheet and have the doctor and the patient sign it when the exam is over. This sheet includes your proposed treatment plan and all treatment options and fulfills the requirements of Delta Dental for informed consent. The day of records and treatment start, you can also print out your formal paperwork and have the patient and doctor sign the final treatment that the patient has chosen. You may also have your patient sign electronically.

Send the diagnosis and treatment plan communication letters to dental colleagues as soon as possible. Calls can also be made during or after the exam to other treating dentists and specialists to relay patient treatment plan information and to check on hygiene and dental health status. Your referring dentists need this verification and the information that they are facilitating the highest quality care option for their patient.

Preparation is the Key to Success

> *Without a clear picture of the customer,*
> *no business can succeed.*
> —Michael E. Gerber

Only by rehearsing will you be able to deliver a fabulous new patient experience. Have your new patient process outlined. Add to this the love that you feel for your profession and your warmth will be naturally expressed. Act with the conviction that you will deliver the best dental care to your new patient. Tell them you will take great care of them and guarantee satisfaction. Don't leave it to chance. You want to do things right every time.

Take the Lead

> *Please influence me now!*
> *I can't make up my mind,*
> *so please help me!*
> —Jordan Belfort

Do you know a dentist who is "able to sell ice to an Eskimo?" I once discussed treatment coordination with a seasoned professional, Mrs. Livvie Matthews, an online marketing business coach from Charlotte, North Carolina. Livvie had worked as a treatment coordinator for fifteen years. She shared her doctor's "secret sauce." When his exam was done, he would confidently say, "Livvie, schedule Mrs. Jones to start treatment tomorrow at 3:30 p.m."

The patient said "Yes" almost every time! This doctor took the treatment coordination lead. He knew the next available appointment time before the new patient exam and his goal was to fill it. The remarkable thing was, that, most of the time, his method worked!

So after meeting with Livvie, I returned to my practice and I tried this "take action" technique. At the end of my orthodontic examination, I confidently said, "Gwen, let's get Sally Sue started with initial records now." To my amazement, it worked! A very high percentage of the next twenty-five new exam patients immediately began treatment! I couldn't believe it! This "take action" approach changed my practice life forever and it can change yours, too! Ask and you shall receive. All you need is a dash of daring.

We Will Take Great Care of You

Do something that says, "I took time to get to know you and I'm acknowledging my appreciation for your business."
—Jeffrey Gitomer

New families are looking for reassurance that choosing your office is the right decision. Give the patient your promise that you will take great care of them. Close the exam with appreciation.

Chapter 4

ADVOCACY

The future belongs to the high achiever,
it belongs to those who act.
                    —J. W. "Bill" Marriott, Jr.

S enior management at Coca Cola Company once made a statement to their employees, "If you are not developing our product, selling our product, or promoting our product, you better have a good reason for being here." Likewise, everyone on your dental team needs to know your services inside and out. They need to be tireless advocates of the doctor and the dental office services.

Office advocacy begins with the first phone call. It next extends to printed materials sent to the potential new patients. It continues with the first welcome, through sales closure, and during treatment. It especially applies when asking current patients to refer more new patients. Speaking and acting on behalf of the practice never ends.

THE WELCOME PACKET
Practice advocacy begins with the informational materials that you send. When the new patient calls to schedule an appointment, it is time to mail and/or email your welcome packet, which must be high quality, up-to-date, welcoming, and attractive. You want to create the feeling of anticipated

excitement. The contents reflect that you care and that you pay attention to detail.

This initial Welcome Packet may include:

1. An office brochure with current photos of you and your team as well as the doctor's family
2. A welcome letter with the time and date of the initial exam
3. A health history form
4. An informational sheet entitled, "Why Choose Our Office"

KNOW YOUR PRODUCTS

> *Don't find customers for your products,*
> *find products for your customers.*
> —Seth Godin

Recently, I visited my dermatologist, Dr. Robert Beer, at Balfour Dermatology in Brentwood, California, for my annual birthday facial with dermabrasion. As I checked in at the front desk, I noticed a framed list of all services he offers. I read down the list of seven items from Botox˚ to lip filler. I was intrigued by a new procedure for fat reduction. I said to myself, "I didn't know he offered that!"

To be an office champion, one must know all of the products and services that are available. You can display these treatments and products at check-in, as well as in your patient display books, which can also be given to your referring doctors to display in their offices. These services can be described on your website, on social media, in your external marketing efforts, in all print literature, on fact sheets, and in brochures, articles, and videos.

As an orthodontist, I have twenty-five products and services that I offer. It is my purpose to highlight everything that I do so that I can help my patients be happier, healthier, and live a better life. I want the whole world to know about our capabilities. Therefore, I am listing them here in this book! You can make a similar outline, which your team can know by heart.

Orthodontic Services:

1. Primary dentition treatment of functional shifts and crossbites
2. Phase I mixed dentition treatment of crowding and growth discrepancies
3. Phase I treatment of thumb-sucking
4. Phase I treatment for mesiodens with impacted central incisor
5. Phase II treatment of tooth alignment
6. Comprehensive treatment non-extraction
7. Comprehensive treatment extraction
8. Comprehensive treatment for impacted canines, bicuspids, and second molars
9. Surgical orthognathic treatment for bite and facial esthetics
10. Treatment of sleep apnea
11. Interdisciplinary orthodontics for implants or bridges
12. Interdisciplinary orthodontic treatment for veneers or crowns
13. Interdisciplinary orthodontic treatment for periodontics
14. Short-term orthodontic treatment pre-restorative or anterior alignment
15. Invisalign
16. Temporomandibular disorder treatment with splint
17. Limited treatment with spring clip aligners (Inman retainers)
18. Limited treatment with clear aligners or overlays
19. Limited treatment with braces for forced tooth eruption
20. Teeth whitening
21. Sports guards
22. Nightguards for bruxism
23. Removable retainers
24. Fixed retainers
25. Positioners

You can have the list of all services displayed in your office. Make sure that your team knows the benefits of each treatment and what can happen if these recommendations are not accepted by the patient. These concepts can be readily explained in lay language. A handy "check-box" menu of possible selections will save a tremendous amount of doctor time and make your front desk exit process seamless. This will also help you tremendously with charges. Now, everyone on your team can be a service advocate!

Four Treatment Coordination Actions

*They don't care how much you know until
they know how much you care.*
—Lou Holtz

Four actions are a must for the treatment coordination process: hearing, translating, evaluating, and revisiting. Here are helpful hints for each.

1. Hearing

You can't listen effectively if you are talking. Ask yourself, "What is most important to my new patient?" Hear with all of your senses. Interpret what the new patient is telling you. Analyze their words, movements, facial expressions, and silences. Ask yourself, "What is their hesitation to starting treatment now? Is it the cost, speed, excellence, location, doctor, or convenience? What is the new patient and their family seeking?"

2. Translating

Get to the core of your patient's truth by asking questions. Be sure what is said is what is meant. Don't make up excuses or imply something different than what the patient has told you. Ask as many questions as you can. Be sure you understand and translate what your patient is telling you.

3. Evaluating

Amazing things will happen when you listen to the consumer.
—Johnathan Mildenhall

Verify that what the patient has told you is true, especially if you are considering a lower cost of services to ensure the start of treatment. Compare and know what is happening in your community. Ask, "Could you bring the offer sheet from the other exam?" Verify the facts.

A private office may choose not to compete with the discount clinic down the street. Make sure you are comparing apples to apples when it comes to discussing services. This is an important part of patient education.

Agree upon arrangements that are within the range of possible for your patient. When this is achieved, it's time to celebrate. You have a new patient to welcome into your practice family.

4. REVISITING

Everything you do must deliver value to the patient and address their spoken and unspoken desires. For patients who do not immediately start treatment, revisit the initial exam. Invite them back for a consultation and discussion. Most "yes" decisions are made in person, face-to-face, in the office.

Gather more information on new patients who don't start the same day. Find out why they did not schedule. Stay in communication and continue to build the relationship. Discover more about what this patient truly wants.

When you welcome a new patient to your office or "close the deal," ask for referrals. This is when your new patient is excited about your office and would love to tell others about their experience. When you feel you have a good relationship, ask: "Are there other family members or friends who need our services? We would love to have more new patients just like you!"

Chapter 5

INFLUENCE

*The highest achievers spent more time
crafting what they did and said
"before" making a request.*
—Robert Cialdini

Why do people buy dentistry? Except for dental pain requiring a root canal or a cracked tooth necessitating extraction, dentistry is viewed as elective.

Your business fulfills a need. In most cases, it is the desire for wellness. You provide the solution to a patient's dental problem. It is your job to figure out quickly your patient's true desire. Focus on this need. Identify the chief complaint. Give the new patient what they request. You haven't much time. The initial exam is usually over in only one hour.

At the end of the first visit, your goal is to reach a "Yes!" decision. In order to achieve this result, it is your task to get the patient to think and feel: "I like this person. I like this office. I trust in their care. I want to have my dental treatment done here—as soon as possible."

PERSUASION

In his book *Pre-suasion*, psychologist Robert Cialdini describes six universal principles of influence including reciprocity, authority, scarcity, social proof, consistency, and likeability. Let's go through these tenets one by one and ponder how they apply to kick-starting the treatment coordination process.

1. RECIPROCITY

> *People say yes to those they owe.*
> —Robert Cialdini

It's Valentine's Day. Your patient relays how happy they are with their newly completed dental treatment. You reciprocate the compliment by giving them a small box of chocolates. The moment is right. You ask for a five-star review. The patient replies, "Certainly" and then does it. Humans are wired with an evolutionary propensity for reciprocity.

Free gifts work. Shoppers at a candy store are 42% more likely to make a purchase if they receive a free sample. Studies have shown that when restaurant wait staff offer a chocolate with the bill, tips will increase by 3.3%. When the diner is invited to take two pieces of candy, tips go up 14.1%. But when the waitress walks away after the first chocolate, then returns to the table with the second chocolate, her tips will climb an astonishing 21.3%! The message here is clear: deliver unexpected delights. But there's another element at play here, the principle of reciprocity: people return favors to those to whom they are indebted.

The rule of reciprocation implies that those who give, get. The receiver doesn't want to feel like a user, taker, freeloader, or cheapskate. It is in our human nature that when we have received something, we want to give back. A sense of indebtedness makes reciprocity work.

Let's take this a step further. Imagine that a candy store clerk asks, "Which is **your favorite** chocolate?" and then provides a free sample. *Customization* is, by definition, the highest form of customer service. Further value is added to the reciprocity transaction.

Food is a formidable source of influence. Studies have shown that food-related gifts can positively affect purchase decisions by as much as 24%. So why not incorporate these findings into your dental practice? Put out snacks for your new patients and families to enjoy. It makes good psychological sense.

Dr. Christopher Phelps, DMD, CMCT (Cialdini Method Certified Trainer) states that only 5– 15% of people given a true gift of value won't reciprocate. That means 85–95% of those given a gift will return the favor. That's a true win-win.

There are many unexpected gifts we can give our new and established patients. Children can pick a toy from the prize box. Adults can receive a whitening tray, a new toothbrush, an oral hygiene goodie bag, sugarless gum, or lip balm at the front desk. These delightful surprises register favorably in the minds of our patients, helping to retain them as loyal customers for life.

2. COMMITMENT

> *Trust is built with consistency.*
> —Lincoln Chafee

We shop at the same grocery store. We attend church services and sit in the same seat. We eat repeatedly at our favorite restaurant because we feel comfort and a sense of belonging. Familiar places consistently do what we expect them to do. The bedrock of commitment is consistency.

Choosing the same place gives us one welcome luxury: we don't have to think through the pros and cons of our decision. Stubborn consistency allows us to not expel mental energy on the unknown. Consistency is a short-cut to the complexities of modern-day life.

The same holds true for dental patients. If they are referred by a friend who has found your office to be consistently good, the new patient will have less decision making in the choice to come to your office.

We want our patients to know that we will do what we say we will do and that we have always done so in the past. We promise to fulfill our dental commitments. We employ this system of consistency to patient confirmations, which increase the likelihood of attendance. The script should go something like this: "I'm calling to remind you of your appointment tomorrow. We'll mark you down as coming then, okay?" (Pause for confirmation and the response, 'Yes.') "Thank you." This tiny commitment-inducing choice of wording can increase attendance by as much as 12%.

Patients want to consistently see the same assistant and doctor. The commitment to long-term employment is looked upon favorably by our patients. Our commitment to maintain consistency in what we deliver gives our patients a feeling of ease and comfort about returning to our office and recommending us to others.

3. SOCIAL PROOF

You may say that I'm a dreamer, but, I'm not the only one
—John Lennon

Social proof starts the minute a new patient enters your office. They see the beautiful smiles of many successful cases on the wall of fame. During the exam, you hand them a beautifully embossed leather folder of before-and-after photos for them to view and hold. As they flip through the pages they exclaim: "I know her. She's my cousin!"

Social proof comes in many forms. It may start with having a reception area filled with happy patients. The new patient may recognize a classmate, friend, or co-worker, which validates the choice in your office. You may want to call attention to the number of patients you have successfully treated to add to your social proof repertoire.

Social proof labels include "a best seller," "most popular," or "most frequently chosen." Use these terms during your exam. Try "Veneers are the **most desired** restoration," or "Clear braces and aligners are **most popular** with adults." These statements give the new patient reassurance that their choice is a good one.

Google is perhaps the number-one social proof site in the nation. Patients go to Google to read your office reviews. Your Google "My Business" profile and reviews need to be as good as possible.

Yelp often becomes a venting site for difficult, unreasonable, attention-seeking, negative, or even mentally ill individuals. Sadly, these reviews are given top priority by Yelp. For this reason, Yelp is most unpopular with dentists. In addition, a corporate dental provider is advertising opposite your reviews. How frustrating! An upset patient is one hundred times more likely to leave a negative review than a happy one. Supportive reviews tend to be put into the "Not Recommended" off-page section of Yelp, while the bad reviews get top-page priority. This is why it is of utmost importance to encourage satisfied patients to write reviews.

Tip the odds further in your favor by seeking *five-star* reviews from happy patients. You can try using an automated service like Podium to email and text your best patients to ask for reviews on Google and Facebook. Yelp reviews need to be requested face-to-face.

If you get new five-star reviews, it's a happy day. A review less than five stars needs to be addressed as soon as possible. Whatever the situation, face it head on. Rectify the problem as best you can with the hope that a review less-than five stars can be improved or taken down.

Social proof also exists on Facebook and Instagram. New patients will be looking at comments and photos of their friends. You want prospective patients to see your smiling, happy patients. Needless to say, the doctor and the entire team should be smiling as well. And don't forget that your Facebook business site includes Facebook recommendations where patients can leave comments.

Although not a review site, new patients will also look at your Instagram to get a social proof "feel" for you and your practice. Stay positive. Photos verify that you and your office are the type that people would like to visit. Even the number of your Instagram followers is social proof. Instagram is extremely popular with the under-forty crowd.

One powerful social proof is the fullness of your reception room. Team members may try to get new patients seated in exam rooms as quickly as possible, but a full waiting area is a good thing when it comes to first impressions. This brings up our next persuasive influence, scarcity.

4. SCARCITY

A lack of scarcity creates a lack of importance.
—Angus Pryor

Your office appointments are limited. It is in the patient's best interest to reserve their treatment time today so that treatment can be started before your schedule is full for the month. The doctor's appointment slots fill quickly.

When we realize that we have gotten to the very last cupcake in the box, it becomes precious. So is the last appointment of the day. Let patients know, "This is the last opening I have today" or: "This is the last availability I have this week. Do you want me to save it for you?"

People assign more importance to opportunities when they are less available. Scarcity increases value. Start by saying: "Many new patients are choosing our office. The doctor is very popular. We have a limited number of appointment times available. Do you prefer 3:00 p.m. tomorrow or 10:00 a.m. next Thursday?"

Know your next available appointment time and make it your mission to fill it to avoid opportunity cost. Always try to have your next scheduling patient take your next opening.

Special offers are also limited. You may be offering free teeth whitening to coincide with new patient exams during the month of May, but this special offer will end the Friday before Mother's Day. This "limited-time offer" will prompt your patients to take action now and pursue their prize.

The same holds true for scarcity sales at dental conventions. We see a new product on the exhibit hall floor. We want it. We know we will never again have this special offer of "no setup fee" or "the lowest monthly payment," so we take action. It is human nature to take action prompted by scarcity of opportunity.

5. AUTHORITY

A credible authority possesses the combination of two qualities: expertise and trustworthiness.
—Robert Cialdini

Your patients will be asking themselves two questions: Is this doctor truly an expert? How truthful can we expect this authority to be? The answers to these two questions will be backed by evidence, including your years of experience, your photos of before-and-after cases, your degrees on the wall, and the management, appearance, and customer service of your office.

As a dentist or specialist, you want to be seen as an authority in the procedures you provide. Your evidence of authority builds trust. The title of doctor, alone, lends authority. The white jacket and a dress or shirt and tie set you apart from the team. Seeing the white jacket builds confidence. You want to project the appearance of authority.

If you are a dental specialist, you have credentials that include degrees from residency programs and thousands of hours of training under the mentorship of experts in the specialty. Your patients will be looking for proof of these experiences, including Board Certification, on your exam room walls. Patients are sufficiently sophisticated to see right through a plaque that attests to completion of an industry-sponsored weekend course. Sketchy accolades can backfire and damage a reputation.

Communicating the limitations of treatment is seen as honest. Trust is enhanced by full disclosure of even mildly negative aspects of the treatment plan. Patients want their dentist to present information to depict reality. Here are a few examples of truthful statements:

> Yes, it is expensive, but your comprehensive dental treatment is important to your tooth longevity, health, and happiness.

> Yes, our treatment fees are not the lowest; however, you will recoup them quickly due to the quality and diminished likelihood of retreatment.

HOW MUCH WILL THIS TREATMENT BE WORTH TO YOU TEN YEARS FROM NOW?

Your new patient is looking for decision-making guidance. Help them by offering your professional judgment. "Now is the time to get started with your dental treatment to prevent this situation from getting worse. Let's schedule your first appointment." You can also state, "If I were you, or if you were my son or my daughter, this is the treatment that I would most highly recommend." Your level of knowledge, experience, and wisdom assures your patients that you are directing them toward what's in their best interest. This is especially true when they cannot decide on their own what to do.

6. LIKABILITY

Pay your patient a compliment, and do it sincerely.
—Ashley Latter

How we approach meeting someone for the first time determines our own level of likability.

The good news is that we have a choice to smile and present a likable attitude. Favorable demeanors include being positive, warm, humorous, enthusiastic, welcoming, empathetic, confident, motivated, engaged, calm, patient, kind, helpful, honest, cheery, polite, and interested. Your actions will control your level of likability.

It is difficult not to like someone who loves you. Liking often grows to love, in the fraternal sense. With each patient I see in my orthodontic office, I start the new patient conversation with something that I like about them. My hope is that I will make each person feel special, liked, and even loved. I want my patients to feel good about themselves and about the experience of coming to my office and to leave my office feeling happier than when they arrived

Start by giving your patient something to smile about. A smile is a silent signal which conveys, "I like you." Likability grows with similarity. We like people who remind us of ourselves. This is why having a patient questionnaire to help you find some connection between you and your new patient is effective. The patient may feel at home in your office if you find something in common. They may think: "I like it here. These people are just like me."

The simple phrase "I like you," will work magic. There is undoubtedly something that we appreciate about each patient we meet. Tell them what it is. "We like you; you always make us laugh." And, who doesn't like food? If your dental office is associated with doughnuts, your patients will have a positive association. Some offices bake chocolate chip cookies. This aroma inspires positive memories of Mom or the bakery at Walt Disney World.

Cooperation and harmony in working together increase likability. This common goal can be dental health. It's important for your patient to realize: "We're in this together. Let's work together toward your dental health goals." Making new friends is a powerful business growth strategy. Be likable. Help your patients feel good about themselves, thereby liking you throughout the entire treatment process.

ELIMINATE THE DISLIKE

I never met a man I didn't like.
—Will Rogers

In 2019, the New England Patriots won the Super Bowl. It was the sixth Super Bowl win for legendary quarterback Tom Brady. Even though Brady is one of the greatest football players of all time, opposing fans still give him a hard time. One day, a young boy asked him what to do with negative fans. Brady replied, "Love them." This is the response of a true champion.

It is an art to hug your haters. It takes determination to look at someone who just gave your dental office a one-star review on Yelp, has emotional needs, and has hurt you, and say to yourself: "This hurtful action is a cry for help. I need to give them just a little more love."

The definition of a professional is one who puts the interests of clients above their own. As dentists, it is our duty to serve patients and their families without judgment. We are there to treat them and help them. This is easier said than done when there is cause for dislike.

I once reminded a treatment coordinator, "If you don't like certain patients, and if you believe that it is not your calling in life to serve them, then you are in the wrong job." Patients can be very demanding. They may ask for special favors or demand extra time to answer a long list of questions. The treatment coordinator cannot be in a "dislike" state of mind. She must be in a "How may I help you?" frame of mind. In the situation mentioned, the treatment coordinator eventually left her job in favor of working in a corporate cubicle.

There is a human tendency for people to dislike those who bring bad news, are demanding of our time, or make us do things that we'd rather not do. Some patients are less likable than others. Professionally, it is our duty to suppress dislike and serve every patient with kindness.

There will be dental patients who dislike us. This is not the fault of the doctor or team. When you deliver bad news, such as the need for a root canal or a past due payment, you become associated with the patient's feelings about the news itself. Always be as kind as possible, so as to minimize the temptation to "shoot the messenger."

Some patients will get angry when reminded that they owe you money. They may associate you and your office with this negative situation. This is why it is best to first send a collection "friendly reminder" statement in the mail rather than call.

It's your choice to adopt a winning attitude of likeability for treatment coordination success. Eliminate attitudes such as anger, impatience, disrespect, conceit, pessimism, suspicion, and boredom. These feelings are useless in the treatment coordination arena. Sing the Bing Crosby song: "Accentuate the positive, eliminate the negative."

Ask the Most Important Question

Sales are contingent upon the attitude of the salesman,
not the attitude of the prospect.
—William Clement Stone

Now say the three magic words, **"Let's get started."** This is the critical step to treatment coordination success. Citizens who are asked, "Will you be voting?" are 25% more likely to cast a ballot. People in general feel compelled to say, "Yes." At the end of each new patient exam, test your influence. Ask the all-important question: "Would you like to start your treatment in our office today?" Go for it. Then keep score.

Part Two

CONVERSION

Sales. It boils down to one word.
Yes!
—Jeffrey Gitomer

Orthodontists are obsessed with case conversion—simply put: "sales." Yet, we never use this word. We talk about percentage of new patients who begin care. The success of our practice, the number of new cases, rests on marketing, new exams performed, and "conversion," the heart of the treatment coordination process. At this intersection lies one word: "Yes."

Marketing makes the phone ring. The office "dream team" arranges for the first appointment. The doctor completes the diagnosis and treatment plan exam. And the coordinators present the financial options. Now comes the moment of truth: do your systems work? Does your new patient start treatment?

Conversion rates in dentistry are never 100%. Patients pay, and some will want their insurance benefits verified first to determine their exact financial obligation. To expedite the decision-making process, secure the insurance information prior to the initial exam. Otherwise, obtain coverage upon arrival and have a team member verify benefits in real time so that the EOB can be factored into the payment contract. Other dental procedures or medical clearance may be needed first. Your thoroughness clearing obstacles and your ability to present the value of care, will determine whether your new patient gets to "Yes!"

Chapter 6

COMMUNICATION

Communication
-the human connection-
is the key to personal and career success.
—Paul J. Meyer

Your paramount key to success is in starting new procedures now. Yet, so few of us in our day-to-day practice of dentistry are fully cognizant of our vital goal. The doctor may be putting out some small fires. The treatment coordinator may be worried that she is running behind. And the back clinical team may be calling the doctor to return to established patients. The centrality of conversion is lost as our minds shift to the past, or begin to worry about the future, or fret about mini-crises of the moment.

If we train ourselves instead to communicate the power of same day starts, immediate success will build staff confidence and reassure patients about the onboarding process. Even a one-day delay in starting makes the process harder. It only becomes that much more difficult every day thereafter.

The communication that you have with your new patient upon first meeting will establish your relationship. Trust will be built and the value of your dental treatment presented. It is now up to you to close the deal. By following up the very next day, you re-establish the emotional commitment of the patient.

With each communication, you are reaffirming your office's expertise. Your willingness to be your patient's top choice dental health provider is expressed personally. You are showing that you will do whatever is necessary to help them receive the care they deserve. Follow-up contacts demonstrate that you are willing to do whatever it takes today, tomorrow, and every day to take great care of them and optimize their results.

ASK QUESTIONS

Success in negotiating is all about maintaining
control in a conversation,
and the person in control is always the
person who is asking the questions.
—Phil M. Jones

You are on a mission to gather information from your new patient. Who? What? When? Where? Why? How? Get specific. Make it a rule to never ask a "say-no" question. Yes and no responses are not what you're after (except the ultimate "Yes!" to treatment, of course).

In your quest for answers, find out what is most important to your patient. Is it cost, quality, or convenience? Look to serve their wants and needs confirming that they have come to the right place.

FOUR TYPES OF QUESTIONS

1. DISCOVERY QUESTIONS
   a) What brings you in today?
   b) What do you want to change about your smile?
   c) What keeps you from smiling?
   d) What can I do to get you to love your smile?

These questions are all great openers for the initial exam process.

2. LEADING QUESTIONS
   a) Do you believe you would eat better with implants?
   b) Are you smiling as much as you would like with the current appearance of your front teeth?
   c) Are you happy with the shade of your front teeth?
   d) Have you had any pain from your wisdom teeth?
   e) Do you presently have any tooth sensitivity?
   f) Does your bite feel comfortable?
   g) Do you believe your life would be better if you straightened your teeth?
   h) Have you ever considered implants with dentures?

These questions lead the conversation to dental services and open it up as to what changes the patient would most like to make.

3. INVOLVEMENT QUESTIONS
   a) How would you feel if you had the smile of your dreams?
   b) Can you imagine how good you will feel when your treatment is completed?

If there is one thing that I hope my readers will remember from this book, it is these involvement questions. People make decisions on what feels right first. Get the patient excited about their future dental treatment! By introducing a future scenario of "How would you feel if…?" or "Can you imagine how good you will feel…?" you allow your patient to create a picture of their future emotions that would be triggered by a "yes" decision. Let them imagine how good it will feel to have the smile of their dreams.

4. CLOSING STATEMENTS AND QUESTIONS
   a) Let's get started with your treatment today.
   b) Let's get started with your records today.
   c) Would this week be a good time for you to begin?
   d) Is it important for you to get started?

Many people never start treatment because they are never prompted or asked! At every initial exam, ask the patient point blank if they would like to get to begin now. Make it your goal to schedule the next appointment, without delay.

Big Case, Big Decision

Some dental cases are complicated, multidisciplinary, comprehensive treatment plans that require coordination amongst several specialists as well as large investments for the patient. Orthognathic surgery is one example. It changes not only the smile and bite but facial form. It requires communication and approvals between doctors.

In such circumstances, it is helpful to remind the patient how they look will affect how they feel, who they date, who they marry, what kind of job they get, and ultimately how successful they are in their career and in life. You can show them a morphed photo of their facial change. Pictures are powerful. Help your patient envision themselves owning the benefits of their surgical, orthodontic, or dental care. When you describe your treatment in human terms, patients are eager to get underway.

Full-mouth reconstruction is also life-changing dentistry. You may want to present your patient with a diagnostic wax-up of their expected result. You may want to provide a smile makeover photo. Show-and-tell in a tangible way the potential for personal transformation.

The Financial Presentation

Your computer system will not close the deal, financially or otherwise. You must do it yourself, person-to-person. The majority of sales are made face-to-face. You need to present the information in an easy-to-understand, non-threatening format.

Here are straightforward scripts to promote the start of care:

We offer three payment options here.

The first option is payment in full, either by cash, check, or credit card today, with a savings of $300 for full orthodontic treatment, or outside financing of CareCredit* with no additional savings.

The second option is a down payment of 25-30%, and financing at 0% interest over a period of months. Does that work for you?

A third possibility is our lowest amount down payment: $X. I'd like to offer you X months at 0% financing. That would give you an interest-free monthly payment of $X. Might that be preferable to you?

Ask, "Which option works best for you?" and wait for the response. Don't speak. Remain silent.

Note that these three options—paying the entire bill immediately, making a standard down payment, or avoiding a large upfront cost—cover the range of possibilities. Presenting three choices and asking, "Which option works best for you?' eliminates a "yes" or "no" response. The decision is **which** option to choose. And the magic words, "Of these three options, what's going to be easier for you?" helps people pick a choice.

The patient and/or family have the chance to indicate their choice. The selection can be displayed on the SimplConsult iPad and also e-mailed. The contract can be easily printed out. Yes! You're ready to get started! Shake hands on this win-win. Time to celebrate!

Once the patient or a responsible family member has selected a personalized payment plan, walk them to your financial coordinator to complete the paperwork for signature. If possible, collect the down payment and start that day or as early as is convenient. It's that easy.

When the Patient Can't Afford Your Payment Plan

What do you do if the patient cannot afford your down payment or a monthly payment plan? Offer CareCredit° or third-party financing. If this fourth option is chosen, **Great!** They can also get started today!

Some patients do not know how to sign up for CareCredit°. Have your financial coordinator help with the Care Credit° application process in the office. Often, by taking action that day, you can get an immediate answer, and still be able to begin care.

When the Patient Asks for a Discount

The patient may ask you, "Can I have a discount?"

The answer is Yes! "You can pay in full and get a $X discount!"

There are other occasions when the doctor may choose to provide a reduced fee as a professional courtesy. It might be the second or third family member or for military personnel. After a period of vesting, staff and their family might qualify—at the doctor's discretion—for a reduced rate or even complimentary care as a work benefit. Whatever your policy regarding discounts, have them documented in writing and understood by the entire team.

THE TEST CLOSE

After you've presented your diagnosis and treatment plan as well as your financial arrangements, now it is time to ask the test close question: "How are you feeling about your payment plan?"

If your patient responds, "It sounds good." Respond with "Good, let's get started." If they react with delay, excuses, or the famous "Let me think about it," ask "What is preventing you from getting started today?" Find out what is truly causing hesitation.

ASK FOR THE CLOSE NOW

> *Ask, and it will be given;*
> *seek, and you will find;*
> *knock, and the door will open.*
> —Mathew 7:7

If you believe that this prospective patient is a good fit for your practice, ask in a professional manner to start treatment today. **Never leave the initial exam without asking the patient if they would like to begin treatment.** Many people never schedule care because they are never asked!

Emphasize that, by providing this treatment, you can improve their life and they will be happier and healthier. Convince the family that your office is absolutely the best place for them to receive care. No one will take better care of the patient than you and your dental team! So it's time to get started! As is true with all sales, the treatment coordinator must live by the ABC mantra: Always Be Closing.

Round out the deal by saying, "I sincerely feel that the decision to start treatment as soon as possible is in your best interest. Let's schedule your next appointment."

Know Your Next Available Appointment Time

The next opening is something everyone in the office must know and work towards filling, especially the doctor. Take action! For example, before leaving the exam room, say to your patient, "You can start today at 2:30 pm. Is this a good time for you?"

Work with your front desk scheduler to maximize the potential of each day. Appointment openings can be reviewed at the morning huddle. The date and time of your next booking opening must be at the top of everyone's mind and computer screen.

Scheduling initial records, imaging, photos, and study models or a scan may take twenty minutes. You want this experience to be unrushed and a good one. You also don't want the patient to have to wait weeks to get underway. Take the time to schedule these tasks as soon as possible.

Same Day Starts

Nothing feels better and grows a practice faster than beginning the case the same day that the patient comes in for the initial exam. Congratulations! You did it! It's a great day in the office!

Orthodontist Jamie Reynolds points out that the conversion rate for same-day starts is naturally 100%. He also estimates that an elite level of same day starts is 50% of all initial exams. That is your goal! Adjust your schedule to be maximally flexible. Obviously, the higher your same-day starts, the higher your overall conversion rate.

Same Day Commitment

Unless a commitment is made, there are only promises and hopes; but no plans.
—Peter F. Drucker

Perhaps the patient cannot start treatment that day or maybe you have absolutely no room in your office schedule. You may be able to at least continue with onboarding by having the financial paperwork signed and the down payment made. This signals a commitment from the patient that they are ready, willing, and able to begin.

To improve your same day closure, do not use the word "contract" for your financial arrangements. Use the terms "paperwork," "agreement," or "form." The word "contract" conjures up images of a binding legal document with consequences that may not be pleasant. Aim for a non-threatening pleasant commitment.

Most patients are probably thinking, "Never sign anything without careful consideration." Use friendlier words, asking them to "approve," "authorize," "endorse," or "okay" their paperwork, agreement, or form. These words are more likely to produce positive associations that make your patients feel comfortable about getting started.

SAME DAY SCHEDULE

Your exam has gone well. The payment method is on file and the patient has said "yes" to treatment. The follow-up visit has been booked. But hold on! It is still possible that the patient may cancel.

Buyer's remorse may set in when the patient speaks to their neighbor, who might tell them that their treatment was less expensive, or perhaps Mom asks Dad for the down payment. Orthodontist Jamie Reynolds reports that 80% of patients who schedule the same day follow through. That means 20% of your best prospects will end up cancelling! Continued constant contact provides the best means to ensuring a smooth and seamless on-boarding process.

Chapter 7

QUALIFYING

*The key to business success is
being in the right place at the right time,
recognizing that you are there,
and taking action!*

—Ray Kroc

If you have a patient in your chair, you are already successful in treatment coordination. Ask yourself, "Why did the last ten patients say yes?" Build on that. Capture and repeat your successful habits.

During the initial exam, you want your new patient to feel that they are in the right place, at the right time. You need to convince your patient to take action and achieve optimal dental health. The need for your dental procedures will not go away. Your task as the doctor or treatment coordinator is to make the value of your dental services readily understood.

The treatment coordination process makes apparent the relief of dental problems. You can make your patient's life better. Afterwards, they will be happier, healthier, and have more confidence. The patient wouldn't be in your office if they didn't have an interest in your services. It is now time to paint the picture of how wonderful life would be with their dental needs resolved and what this is worth to them over a lifetime.

Keep it simple. Don't waste a minute of your patient's time. Remember, no one will join your office if not asked. In order to schedule the procedure, now comes the moment of truth: "The Close."

Buying Signs

There are many visual and auditory clues as to when the patient is ready to start treatment. Look for these "buying signs." When you see them, it's time to start wrapping up the exam.

- Leaning in
- Conversing warmly
- Smiling
- Reading the paperwork that you have provided
- Viewing the material and products again
- Touching the demonstration product again
- Telling you which treatment they would like

Ask, "How do you feel so far about everything we've discussed?" If there is hesitation, keep talking, educating, and explaining. If the response is "I feel great! I want to get started," then congratulations! Your TC job is done.

Follow Up

> *"Of the options we've offered,*
> *which do you feel would best serve you right now?"*
> —Michael E. Gerber

When the treatment coordinator or, preferably, the doctor, calls the patient two days later, they should give VIP treatment. Perhaps the family needs a 5:00 p.m. appointment. Give it to them. Maybe both parents prefer to come in on a Saturday. It is up to the practice owner to decide how best to accommodate the desires of each prospective new patient.

New patients will appreciate hearing directly from the doctor. The doctor can agree to an additional consultation if another family member has questions. The treatment coordinator can also call to discuss alternative payment options. Your ultimate goal is to get a yes or no answer to starting treatment. If you hear a no, don't quit yet! Find out why and try to work things out

Should the patient not choose to start treatment that day, ask for a good day and time for a follow-up call. Another option would be to politely ask, "Would it be convenient for me to follow-up with you in two days?"

Objections

> *Treat objections*
> *as requests for further information.*
> —Brian Tracy

Many patients do not immediately schedule. They may want to get started but they need reassurance that they are making a wise decision. Some buyers don't want to be hasty. And, they question themselves the minute they leave your office; they are looking for affirmation.

Hesitation is understandable. Buyer's remorse and cognitive dissonance may be factors. These phenomenon occur when two conflicting thoughts happen simultaneously. When making a buying decision, especially if spending a large amount of money, objections arise—even when primed to buy. The biggest factor is usually money.

When you make your follow-up phone calls, find out why the patient hasn't started treatment yet. You can work around most roadblocks only if you know what is causing them. Perhaps it is the down payment, the available appointment times, the overall price, or fear of the procedure. Come up with a solution to the patient's concerns. Eliminate the reason that's holding them back. Confirm that they are making the right choice.

Three Ways Not to Respond to Resistance

> *One of the biggest mistakes dentists make is that*
> *when they get an objection from a patient*
> *they become all defensive and handle the objection badly.*
> —Ashley Latter

If you, as the doctor, get endless questions that you have answered many times, you might become slightly irritated. This might also be the case for the treatment coordinator, who may feel she wants the exam to be over. Do not get anxious or defensive. **Take a deep breath.** Remain calm. Taking extra time will pay off. Maintain control.

When patients take excessive time and you sense that they may do this at every future appointment, you may want to consider imposing a surcharge to their treatment fee. This is reasonable. We call these "high-maintenance" patients.

Here are three things to remember when you feel that the temperature in the exam rising:

1. DON'T GET DEFENSIVE

Doctors let ego pull them into getting defensive. The patient or family may say, "That's too much money," or "Can't you just fix this one tooth?" You may feel insulted. Pleasantly continue the conversation. You might say, "I wish that were possible, however, that is not in your best interest. What I have offered you is the best treatment. Let's discuss how we can give you the best care that you need and deserve."

2. DON'T BECOME AGGRESSIVE

Never let the patient feel as though they are wrong. You have nothing to prove. You are simply there to provide service. Whatever the patient says, no matter how many times you need to explain the procedure, use positive affirmation, even if only to say, "I hear you." Continue discussion in a calm and friendly manner.

3. DON'T GIVE UP

Sadly, giving up is what many treatment coordinators and doctors do as soon as someone makes even one objection. Some doctors and TCs say nothing or, even worse, they say "OK," or, "I understand," and just walk away.

Giving up is the worst reaction of all. Most patients need to be convinced that they are making the best decision moving forward with their dental care. For all you know, they may have considerable interest in getting started and all they need is for you to say the magic words, "Let's get started."

JUSTIFYING TREATMENT DECISIONS

People are more likely to read an advertisement from a major purchase **after** they have bought the product than before. Reading the ad reinforces the correctness of their decision, thus eliminating cognitive dissonance and buyer's remorse. During the first office encounter, give your patient something to read. I would recommend making a custom sheet entitled "Why Choose Us." List all the reasons why your patients should select your practice. Encourage the patient and family members to take a copy home.

The Doctor as Treatment Coordinator

Commit to "CAN I" –
Constant And Never-Ending Improvement.
—Tony Robbins

There are plenty of dentists who do not have a treatment coordinator. The doctor simply does the exam and starts the treatment, often with the aid of a team member who takes notes. The dentist can then escort the patient to the front desk where the financial coordinator writes up the financial agreement.

Start rates can be compared between the doctor and the TC. Sometimes the doctor can benefit from a treatment coordinator. In other circumstances, the doctor is better off doing the initial exam on their own. If the doctor has a near 100% conversion rate performing treatment coordination activities and an appointed treatment coordinator has a 33% conversion rate, then by all means the doctor is better off doing the initial exam on their own.

Developing a treatment coordinator can cost over $25,000. Training can begin with sponsoring attendance at a course and include professional recording or videotaping. Phone skills also need to be polished. You could send your treatment coordinator to a dental office management convention. You might hire virtual consultants. You may even hire a special coach specifically to hone your follow-up phone skills and scripts so as to boost start numbers.

Your treatment coordinator must be capable of getting the job done. Expectations need to be clear from the beginning. Otherwise, you may be in a constant correction, never-ending mode of job development. Make sure your treatment coordinator has the computer resources and bandwidth to make calls, and verbal skills conviction to ensure positive outcomes.

Like the Sino-Japanese philosophy of kaizen, to change for the better, we must plan, do, check, and act to continuously improve all functions which involve all employees from CEO to frontline workers for treatment coordination excellence. Everyone in the dental office can be devoted to Constant and Never-Ending Improvement (CANI). We are all part of the treatment coordination process and must appreciate its constant demands.

Show Me How I Can Afford Dental Treatment

It almost never happens that a patient walks into your dental or specialty practice with $5,000 ready to pay for treatment. As an entrepreneur, you must have the skill to make a deal acceptable to your new patient—to get the financial transaction done. Listening to what the patient wants is the best way to build trust, foster happiness, and grow your business. In the long run, this will save you time and money. You want your onboarding process to be fast, easy, and successful.

When the patient claims finances are holding them back, consider instead that they are telling you, "Show me how I can afford this care." Ask what their objection is; many times the obstacle is financial, and you can agree mutually upon acceptable terms. This is also a valuable opportunity for feedback on how your office's treatment coordination process is doing.

Taking Out the Middleman

It is not fair to ask of others
what you are unwilling to do yourself.
—Eleanor Roosevelt

Have you ever bought a new car? We enter the dealership knowing the car that we want. We look at it. We take it for a test drive. In our minds, we also know what we want to pay. Perhaps we have gone online and looked up what this car is worth or talked to friends and asked what they paid for this style of car. We probably already have a down payment in mind as well as the monthly installment that would fit into our budget.

Car dealers often place us in a circle of uncertainty. They sit us down first with the car salesperson. He tells us the price. We make a counteroffer. He then goes to speak with the "mystery manager" in another room. Maybe this middleman accepts our price; maybe he doesn't. This is the first point at which we have a decision to make—to either accept the deal, bargain more, or walk out.

The salesman might say, "I cannot come down on price, but I can negotiate the terms of financing." This might be OK, so we continue. At this point we may be transferred to yet another person who works out the monetary arrangements.

We do not want our dental patients to feel as though they are in an auto dealership! Get rid of the middlemen! Work out the details surrounding cost right then and there. This can be done very easily if the doctor/owner is directly involved in the financial process when the initial clinical assessment is done. I call this "immediate financial coordination." Financial terms are accepted, the paperwork is signed, the down payment is made, and your patient begins care on the spot. 1-2-3-4.

IMMEDIATE FINANCIAL COORDINATION

I recall one particular new patient exam. A young girl came in with her mom and three siblings, seeking orthodontic treatment. I shared my diagnosis and plan. I explained the estimated length of care and showed them a set of similar before-and-after photos.

I then described the cost of initial records, the standard down payment, and the calculated monthly payment. The mother said the money down was fine and that she could start treatment that day. The monthly rate was also fine. However, the $589 cost of records was unforeseen, and she was not prepared to pay that fee. She wanted to include the initial records charge in the monthly payment plan. So, we added three months to the contract to cover records. This negotiation took less than three minutes.

The initial down payment was made, the contract signed, and the initial records taken. We then worked the patient into the daily schedule to begin care. Everyone was happy—the patient, her mom, the office team, and especially the doctor, who was able to help a family while growing the business.

INITIAL RECORDS

If you are an orthodontic office, your initial records coordinator can help you make follow-up phone calls and, in the process, help fill in her own work schedule. The goal after all, is to schedule initial records. This is your second benchmark: number of initial records.

General dentists and other specialists don't have a separate appointment called "initial records" but orthodontists do. This appointment includes taking extraoral and intraoral photographs, panoramic X-ray, lateral ceph-alometric X-ray, and study models. This appointment usually takes twenty minutes. If you are a general dentist and you take mounted study models or a full-mouth series, you may want to consider scheduling this as a separate appointment.

THE PRICE

The low-cost game is hard to play. There will always be someone less expensive than you and your office. Based on the economics of your neighborhood, set your price and stick to it. This will serve you best in the long run.

Bargain-basement shoppers, in general, are not good patients. They do not want to pay for treatment in the first place and they will be very unwilling to accept the cost of necessary additional services—even for replacement of a lost retainer or additional, needed dental cleaning

Dental schools provide good care at a low price. Patients unable to pay can be referred directly to a nearby school of dentistry. There may be a public assistance clinic in your community. Except for occasional complimentary care or a donated case, those running a small business are not able to give treatment away for free.

I once knew a dentist who built a beautiful office in our community. He was well known, since he had grown up and gone to high school here. His family owned a local restaurant. His biggest challenge was that all of his friends and relatives wanted free or reduced cost dentistry! He was such a nice guy, and it was difficult for him to say, "No." Eventually, he moved away to pursue another aspect of dentistry. I have often wondered if the hometown expectation of discounted care played a major influence on his career decision.

Your price must be stated with confidence, and without hesitation or apology. This is the value of your treatment, the cost of doing business with your office. You can offer multiple payment plans. One of them should be workable for most people. What matters is the patient's ability to pay. Otherwise, your practice is not the best option for them.

SECOND OPINIONS

The competition down the street is not the enemy. When a patient states that they will be going for a second opinion, simply ask, "What will you be looking for?" The answer will usually be, "A lower price."

Even if you feel that another office has inferior customer service, or a poor reputation, don't play the game of negativity. Focus on making your practice and products the best they can be, highlighting how your office is outstanding and the patient's best choice. The patient will see for themselves why it would be best to choose your practice, even if the cost is somewhat higher. Value equals quality divided by cost. Emphasize your value and the quality of your professional care.

Invite the patient back for a re-evaluation after they have gathered all of their diagnoses and treatment plans. Let the patient know that your practice is worth the price, and that you would like to be their top choice dental health-care provider.

IMPOSSIBLE PATIENTS

Speaking to residents in the practice management course at a nearby dental school, I highlighted one patient that every practice should avoid: the multiple opinion (five or more), "I'm OK, **you're not OK**" patient. This negative, fault-finding archetype is outlined in my book, *At Your Service: 5-Star Customer Care for a Successful Dental Practice*. This individual feels they know more than their doctors and finds fault with every dentist and specialist they have ever seen. This interaction will cost you time, money, and grief. In the end, no matter how good the treatment you provide, this patient will leave you a one-star review on Yelp. You must politely but firmly say, "This may not be the right office for you." Beware of the patient that other offices have already turned away!

MISSED EXAMS

Don't give up on individuals who fail their first, or even second, appointment. But missing a third appointment, that's a different story. In this situation, send one final text advising them that they may call for accommodation on the same day of the exam. Beyond that, the "three strikes, you're out" rule of "dismissed" category applies.

A missed exam gives your office the chance to check on the success of your own outreach messaging. Did they receive your pre-appointment phone call, text message, and welcome materials? Why didn't the reminder work best for them? Ask if adequate directions were given. Use the opportunity to improve your own communication systems.

THE PENDING LIST

Should your patient not start or schedule treatment on the day of the exam, change their status to "pending." Designate one person to call and follow up. This is the hard work of treatment coordination. This is where persistence pays off. Adopt the treatment coordination mantra: **We will call the pending patients frequently and consistently. We will not give up until we receive a yes or a no.**

Sales expert Weldon Long claims that the biggest mistake in sales is believing that potential clients will pick up the phone and call back. He states, "There is no Santa Claus or Tooth Fairy, and prospects rarely (if ever) call back!" In sales, a "no" won't kill you. It's the "I don't know, I'll call" that will undermine success, especially if there is no follow-through.

It is not unusual for a patient to seek multiple opinions. You want to be their top choice. Tell them so! Let them know that you care the most. I'm a big advocate of the doctor making at least the first follow-up phone call. It has been proven to me many times that patients will say things to the doctor that they won't say to the TC. The doctor can ask the patient what is holding them back. By fully understanding the patient's needs and limitations, barriers to starting treatment can be eliminated.

SEND A THANK YOU

Whether or not your new patient starts treatment that day, send a thank-you card of welcome following the initial exam. Tell them that you hope that their first visit was enjoyable. Include the dentist's and treatment coordinator's business cards and offer assistance. Tell them that you look forward to seeing them again soon.

Chapter 8

DELAY

A prophecy fulfills itself.
If you assume that they need care now
and want to do this with you,
then you will deal with them accordingly,
and eventually they will become your clients.
—Gavriel Asulin

Some percentage of your new patients will not start treatment immediately. Most will say, "I need to think about it." When you receive this common response, ask, "What will you be thinking about?" Keep asking questions and sharing information. Get to the true reason. Here lies the time-consuming work of treatment coordination. When delay is encountered, your job is to communicate, to build trust and confidence, and to do the necessary work to overcome lingering objections.

Don't take the responses of the procrastinator personally. The patient and their family may be drowning in a sea of uncertainty after the initial exam. Invite them into your safe and secure lifeboat. Help them make the decision to get started.

The Seven Excuses

One of the best predictors of ultimate success...
isn't talent or even industry expertise,
but how you explain failures and rejections.
—Daniel H. Pink

There are seven common excuses for not undertaking dental treatment immediately. They are: price, payment options, convenience, changed my mind, need to talk to spouse/parent, going for more opinions, and need to think. When you hear one of these objections, see it as a positive sign that the patient wants to receive care at your office. That's right, the new patient is interested in your care. If the new patient were apathetic, they would be more likely to say nothing. Think positively. You are 80% on your way to getting started. All you need now is to build that 20% of extra trust and reassurance to get your patient to making the start decision.

1. "It's too expensive"

Dentistry can be life changing. Its value is worth many times what patients pay for it. It is an investment in health, happiness, and success. Paint a positive picture for your patient of the return on their dental investment. Replace the words "cost" or "price" with "benefits."

Directing thoughts to the future long-term benefits is excellent for diffusing money concerns. Try asking: "Ten years from now, will this dental treatment be worth more or less to you than what you are investing in it today?"

Always agree with your client. You can use the response, "Yes, it is a large investment—dental treatments are not cheap. You might add, "I know that our prices are not the lowest, but that's because we provide the best quality care and customer service, and our Board-Certified doctor has thirty years of experience." This question helps the patient get away from immediate monetary thoughts and back to a focus on the benefits, rewards, and the true value of treatment.

Determine what is doable for the patient and their budget. It is up to the owner-doctor whether they are willing to make special financial arrangements. You may want to give a courtesy for payment in full. You may have a special offer for patients beginning care at this time. If your schedule is not completely full and your office has not reached its goal for the month, you may want to create an offer to drive new business.

Gavriel Asulin in his book, *"Turn Your Dental Practice into a Successful Business,"* states that giving clients a discount is one of the most effective tools for closing a deal. We have found over the years that such promotions are effective at the $300 level. If you are offering a comprehensive treatment of several thousand dollars and want an effective call to action or even an incentive for prepayment in full, a $300 courtesy usually gets that job done.

2. "I CAN'T AFFORD IT."

… We can work it out.
—Paul McCartney

Usually the overall price is not the problem in agreeing to procedures. It is the down payment, which should be considered the first move towards achieving dental health. This hesitancy can be overcome by flexible payment plans or third-party financing.

Ask the patient what options they would like to help them get started. Explore together how you can work with their budget to make dental treatment attainable. The individual will believe that they can afford the entire cost only if both the money down and the monthly payment are affordable.

If you offer CareCredit®, show the equal monthly payment amounts. If your new patient envisions this as fitting for them, help them set up CareCredit® financing themselves on their phone right then and there in your office. When you provide this level of service, the patient will be so enthused about their on-site approval that they might just begin treatment that day.

3. "YOU'RE NOT CONVENIENT"

Some patients are willing to travel seven hours for specialty dental treatment. Location is usually not the real problem for the patient who does not start. They drove to your office for the initial exam. They may have experienced traffic delays but they could choose a different appointment time. Perhaps morning would be less hassle for them. Working adults and even some parents bringing children in for care might prefer extra-early times.

When someone says "location" what they might mean is "time spent in the office." Be sure to see patients promptly. Even a patient who lives down the street will be unhappy with prolonged wait times. Consider the entire patient experience when you hear the excuse of "location." Emphasize the positives about your practice, such as your parking lot or extended hours, and be able to provide clients with what they truly want, professionalism and exceptional personal care. Your business days or your hours of operation may be problematic. Ask for clarity on why the patient thinks your office is not "convenient." Perhaps accommodations can be made.

Sometimes office hours are simply not doable for every individual. Perhaps their best day is Saturday but you're not open on weekends. To overcome scheduling barriers, you will need to create a high degree of perceived value. Encourage your patient to amend their schedule to be able to receive the best treatment in your office.

Patients will drive hours and come in on work and school days if they sense the highest quality care. In my personal case, this is often the situation with orthognathic surgery patients. I had someone call my California office from Rhode Island telling me they would like to come to me for orthognathic surgical treatment (I told them this would not be advised and I referred them the maxillofacial oral surgery department at a local dental school.) I have one patient who lives in London doing Invisalign; we do video visits and in person check-ups about once per year. Think outside the box to meet patient demands.

4. "I CHANGED MY MIND."

> *Nothing escapes your customer*
> *as he absorbs the information, he uses*
> *to make his decision to buy or not to buy.*
> —Michael E. Gerber

Do not overwhelm your new patients with too much technical information! After your client hears your diagnosis and treatment plan, it is possible that they will make the decision that they simply are not going to proceed. They may be scared, overwhelmed, or confused. Or, they may not have the money (and be too embarrassed to admit it).

It is your job to reduce uncertainty and build trust. Assure your new patient that they are in the best hands of the best doctor, who has done thousands of these procedures with an excellent success rate. Let your patient know that you can be trusted. Pay attention to their words and actions.

Perhaps the patient heard the procedural steps and is confused. There may be a step they wish to avoid. Ask what they are thinking about the process. Maybe they believe the treatment will take too long. Perhaps they need your office to initiate interdisciplinary care and need your help to arrange all of their appointments. Find out why they feel the way they do. They came in wanting care and something has changed. Ask them what changed their mind.

5. "I NEED TO TALK IT OVER WITH MY SPOUSE."
Great! The next time you hear this response, follow through with this question: "Would you like to call him right now? We (the doctor and treatment coordinator) can leave the room and give you some privacy."

Clarify further the information the patient will be presenting. Maybe the patient needs family agreement on final financial arrangements. The benefits and value of the treatment needs reinforcement. Parents may want to discuss matters alone without their children. Children may also leave the room. Leaving the room and letting families speak amongst themselves often leads to an immediate "yes" decision.

You could ask, "If it's OK with your wife (or husband), would you start treatment today?" You might find out that the partner decision maker is just outside the office, waiting in the car. Invite him or her in. If necessary, arrange to call the spouse at a convenient time. Involve the decision maker. The spouse will most often agree with starting treatment.

6. "I'M GOING FOR MORE OPINIONS."
This decision is often sparked by dentists who give out several referral cards for specialty services. Nowadays, people are convinced that if they have not gone for multiple opinions, that they have not done due diligence. That's understandable. It's a big decision.

At least say, "I'm sure that after you have gone for all of your consultations that you will find that our office is the best place for you. Please come back after you have made all of your comparisons. We will take the best care of you and we want to be your top choice."

If your patient is going for more than one "second" opinion, ask questions about what information has been presented by the other professionals. Ask that they return to your office with their additional paperwork. Make sure that your prospect isn't comparing apples to oranges.

Emphasize the longevity of your practice, years of experience, and number of cases like theirs completed; mention how your office is different and why it's the best. Present your special benefits and value points. Ask: "Is there any additional information or reassurance that I can provide to make your choice easier?" Convince your patient that you will take great care of them.

7. "I NEED TO THINK ABOUT IT."

You're guaranteed to hear this final response from at least twenty percent of new exams. Recognize that this as a stall tactic, which can also be worded in other ways such as:

"I'll call when we're ready."

"We'll review this information and make a decision soon."

"Let me sleep on it."

Some people simply can't decide at first exposure. Agree with them and give a positive response, "Excellent, Mrs. Smith, take your time and think about it."

Here it is worthwhile to initiate another silence to show confidence on the part of your practice and in the quality of your care, customer service, and your price. Respect your client and their wishes. After a brief silent pause while preparing the patient's exam folder, you can wrap up your exam time together by saying: "Is there anything else you would like me to cover?" or "Is there any way I could alter the financial arrangements to help you get started?"

Return to what the patient does want, resolution of their chief complaint. Highlight the benefits again to their dental health, happiness, and well-being from your dental care. Give them a heartfelt thank you, a fond farewell, and tell them you look forward to contacting them again soon and having them as a new patient. Then, call them in two days.

Dental Fear

Anxiety is a common factor in the dental decision-making process. Your patient will most likely never come straight out and tell you that they are scared. Your mission is to eliminate all worries so your patient can proceed with confidence. Whenever prospects delay treatment, consider that it might be fear of the unknown which needs to be addressed.

Remind the patient that you are an expert in your field and have treated thousands of happy patients. Prove that you are patient, gentle, and kind, and that you will guide them through the entire dental process. You will be there for them every step of the way.

Fears include cost, pain, making a mistake, the unknown, lack of knowledge, or third-party stories that they've heard. Fear often originates in a dental memory from childhood.

To overcome anxiety, take things slowly. Put yourself in the patient's place. If you would feel a certain way in their situation, chances are that the patient is feeling that way as well. Ask, "What questions do you have about how this plan meets your needs, or about any of the parts of treatment?"

In some situations, such as orthognathic surgery, you may want your patient to meet another patient who has had the procedure. This is very helpful for building patient confidence. Recorded video testimonials can also help. Before-and-after photos of your previous cases may help the patient imagine their successful result.

D IS FOR "DIFFICULT PATIENT"

> *Dismiss whatever insults your soul.*
> —Walt Whitman

Difficult patients drain your time and resources and add negative karma to your practice. They will annoy your team, doctor, and other very good patients. When you get an extremely troubling vibe at the initial exam, remember that you are under no obligation to accept everyone into your practice. Rudeness to the doctor or the team can never be tolerated. Patients who mistrust you, disrespect you, or (heaven forbid) hang up on your phone call, need to be dismissed as soon as possible.

When a new patient comes in as a third, fourth, or fifth opinion, also beware. Patients may rant about their previous disappointments with other dentists. The individual may ask to have treatment redone. This is a worrisome warning sign. Patients ask for a mirror and point to their teeth with their fingers explaining what needs to be redone and what went wrong. They bring in photos so you can see what their teeth looked like twenty years ago. Your fight-or-flight response signals, "run!", and with good cause.

Beware of the ego response that goes off in your head saying, "But I'm better than these other dentists." Trust your gut. It's not the dentists, it's the patient! Don't let pride override intuition and rationality. D is for dismiss!

Prioritize Your New Patients

Keep notes of what your new patients tell you. You may want to start a "tickle file" or computer notes folder of your top prospects. When they tell you, "I'll start next month" or, "I'll start in the New Year," document that conversation and schedule a follow-up call. Review this list regularly. Make the calls, send postcards, and/or use automated emails or text messages to reignite interest and keep the relationship going.

Set Your Eyes on the Prize

To build a long-term, successful enterprise,
when you don't close a sale, open a relationship.
—Patricia Tripp

As you work toward your monthly numbers, keep calling and scheduling until you achieve them. Deal with and resolve roadblocks for new patients. Build relationships and press on! Persist until the very last hour of the last day of the month. And remember, those who systematically stay in touch with prospective patients do not come across as "pushy," but just the opposite; they are viewed as kind, patient, caring, and dedicated dental professionals who do their job faithfully with excellence.

Chapter 9

FOLLOW-UP

For every sale you miss because you're too enthusiastic,
you will miss a hundred because you're not enthusiastic enough.
—Zig Ziglar

With good patient management software, dentists can generate numerous patient reports, including:

- Failed Exams
- Pending Starts
- Will Call
- Recall or Observation

Whatever you call your unscheduled patient lists, you may have hundreds—if not thousands—of patients right now in your database in one of these four categories in need of your dental services. All that you need to do is call them, stay in touch, or reach out in a special way, and ask them if they have considered getting started.

ELIMINATE FEAR OF ASKING
Not everyone will join your dental practice but **no one** will join if not asked. Eliminate the fear of asking. Tell yourself, "I want to help others. The only

way to do so is to reach out to them and ask." Patients need our services, and the only way we can help them is to ask.

Don't fear rejection. When someone definitively says "**no**," ask why, and then tell them they can always come back to your office for treatment in the future. Then move on to the next patient.

Hot Calls

Action is what separates the winners from the whiners.
—Weldon Long

Make your follow-up call within two days. Let the patient know that you are thinking about them, that you care about them, and that you will take great care of them. You are waiting for their treatment decision. Hot calls made within two days of the initial visit have the highest success rate. Don't let this opportunity slip by. With each passing day, your call becomes colder. Pick up the phone and make something happen.

Saying, "I don't want to be 'pushy'" and not striking while the iron is hot is a copout. Treatment coordination is sales. Period. The more calls you make, the better your odds. It's that simple. Your call becomes less warm the longer you wait. After a month, your call is a bit chilly. After three months, it's cold. Beyond that, it's a freeze. Don't delude yourself by thinking that the new patient will contact you on their own. They won't.

Imagine that you have been on a first date. You're excited about this new person and you can't wait to see them again. But the day after you meet, they don't call. Two days pass. You may be shy, busy, away, or unsure, and you don't reach out either. As the days go by, you feel disappointed, and believe they may never call. You start to forget them.

After three weeks, you finally hear from them. But, by then, the thrill is gone. Your excitement has cooled. Besides, during that week, you met someone else whom you really like, and they called the very next day. Now what?

It's the same way with potential new patients! Perhaps during that week when the treatment coordinator, receptionist, or doctor didn't follow-up, your new patient decided to go for a second opinion. Or, buyer's remorse has set in, and they've decided that their money should go towards a vacation to Disneyland.

Let your new patients know that life is short and there are great benefits to beginning their treatment now. Their condition is not going to go away. In fact, it can only get worse. The problem needs to be taken care of either now or in the near future. You want to be their top choice. And, you will work hard to give them the very best care that they deserve.

In his book, *Turn Your Dental Practice into a Successful Business,* dental business consultant Gavriel Asulin states that two days is the best time to begin follow-ups after the initial exam appointment. Why? Because after visiting the practice, two days is not long enough to do much of anything different regarding the matter. Many patients who want to "think about it" may want to check out alternative practices or price check. But, they do not necessarily have the time or energy to do so. After two days, they realize that it is easiest and best to start with you and they most likely still want to start the treatment. After two days is the perfect time for your new patient to say "yes" to starting treatment.

Warm Calls

I am now a true believer in warm calls being made by the doctor. This was not always my perspective. Many of your new patients who did not schedule care the day of the treatment diagnosis will eventually start treatment. These individuals may schedule during your warm call at two weeks. Why? First of all, it's the doctor on the phone and they know that they need the treatment. They want to proceed; they just needed a reminder and personalized attention to be convinced to start. Secondly, they've talked about it, thought about it, and they may or may not have gone for more opinions. Chances are that other doctor's diagnosis, treatment plan, and cost are comparable. The patient has procrastinated and needs to make a commitment. You're there to help them, and now is their time to start.

So just do it! Follow through. Put down this book right now and start making warm calls. Take the first step. Keep at it until you experience your first positive result. Once you do, you'll be hooked. I guarantee it.

The Opener

Begin always by expecting good things to happen.
—Tom Hopkins

When you make your call, make the prospect think. Be silent and let them talk. The conversation could go something like this:

> Your opener: "Hello! This is Dr. X. How are you today?'
> Your patient hopefully replies: "I'm great! How are you?"
> Your reply: "I'm fantastic! The reason I'm calling is to ask if you've given any more thought to starting your dental treatment?"
> Now:
>> Don't talk ...
>> Just wait ...
>> Count to 30 ...
>> Silence is golden ...
>> Look at your watch ...
>> Whoever speaks first loses ...
> Your patient finally replies: "Yes I have. I would like to begin."
> Your closer: "Great! Let's schedule you for this Tuesday at 1:30 p.m. Would that work for you?"
> Success: "Yes it does."
> It's that easy. Try it.

If your patient answers, "No, I haven't planned on it," then you have two choices. Either remind them about the initial findings and the necessity of coming in for care or invite them for a follow-up visit to further explain the diagnosis and treatment plan.

COLD CALLS

> *A winner is just a loser who tried one more time.*
> —George M. Moore, Jr.

Every day, a team member can be assigned to call patients who have come in for an examination and not yet started treatment. Unless your practice is absolutely full, there is no good reason not to follow-up with unscheduled new patients. Most doctors delegate this important task to one person, perhaps a treatment coordinator, and they assume that it is being done.

Never assume. Print out your pending and Will-call lists right now and see how many names you have on your lists.

Being diligent about your Pending List will determine if your practice grows or declines. Contacting and scheduling these prospects is of primary concern to the doctor and the entire team. An A+ team player making forty or more calls per day will no doubt keep your schedule full. The treatment coordinator should report these terrific results at the weekly team meeting. If this is not the case, doctors need to dig in and complete this essential task themselves.

Spanish Pending List

Se habla espanol.
—Gwendoline Rios, Treatment Coordinator

Do you know that Spanish is the most frequently spoken language in the world? In California, 25% of residents speak Spanish as their primary language. This preference should be indicated in your electronic record system, and whenever possible, an in-office translator should be present. It is helpful to designate who in your office will call and follow-up with non-English-speaking patients. Creating a separate computerized list for this population is key for successful follow-up.

Many automated follow-up systems also offer Spanish. SimplSign from SimplConsult offers free Spanish presentation slides, texts, and emails. I've asked my Spanish-speaking-patients how they like this system, and they say, "Bueno!"

The Power of a Personal Phone Call

A personal phone call still holds more clout than a card, email, or text. It's one caring human being calling another. Thank your new patient individually for considering your office and invite them to schedule treatment now, while you have them on the phone.

Your job is to communicate the value and benefits of dental care and the urgency of maintaining dental health, while building trust that your office is "on it." This is where the full-time job of onboarding begins. Will you adopt a "'til they buy or die" burning desire for success, or will you simply give up? This is the difference between a champion and a run-of-the-mill treatment coordinator: focus, and the grit to stick with the task.

Imagine that you are seeking dental treatment for your child. You visit three dentists. They are all experienced, they all have beautiful and convenient offices, and their teams are all professional, experienced, and friendly. Their costs are comparable, and their quality of treatment and patient experience are all good. You have gone for multiple exams, but only one doctor took the time to call within two days. In addition, they sent you a personal handwritten thank-you note and an email, asking you to call if you had any additional questions. Which practice would you choose?

Follow-up Card

*We wildly underestimate the power
of the tiniest personal touch.*
—Tom Peters

A tailored note is powerful. It demonstrates care and thoughtfulness. We all love receiving a card that expresses gratitude. We hope that our patients will feel the same way about getting an individualized message card from us.

Smart Practice° has a plethora of cards for every possible dental and special occasion. Unlike a phone, email, or text, cards are delightfully tangible. Old-fashioned snail mail reminds the patient that "you care enough to send the very best." It adds value to your service and helps to build your relationship.

A postcard will likely be saved as a constant reminder to call your office. While phone numbers can be changed or incoming calls allowed to go to voicemail, neither rain, nor snow, nor sleet, or hail will keep the postal service from delivering your card. Even if a family moves, cards will be forwarded to their new address. Cards are my second choice for immediate follow-up.

Sending additional information is a good way to keep in touch. Keep families up to date with new offers and services in your office. Remember, your pending patient is always a potential "Yes!"

Follow-up Email

As a busy mother and professional myself, I look at my emails daily, whereas landline voicemails are checked less frequently, maybe once a week. A postcard may take a week to answer. Emails tend to produce an immediate response. For busy families with two working parents, emails are the way to go for follow-up communication.

Emails are also cost-effective. Your front-desk coordinator can send emails, or your office can use an automated service such as SimplConsult for exam follow-up. Emails also tend to prompt an immediate yes or no answer. It is much easier for a prospective patient to say "no" by email than over the phone. If you have not heard from your patient by phone, or in response to a card, send an email.

Follow-up Text

Don't assume that calls, cards, or even emails will reach every patient. Ask specifically during the exam what form of communication they would prefer. You can include this question on your "Getting to Know You" welcome sheet. Many visitors to your office, especially younger ones, will choose texting. If so, great. Text them with forty-eight hours of initial contact

It's said that most people respond to a text within thirty seconds. My office recently signed up for Podium, which enables two-way text messaging from our website to give us an immediate communication with our new and prospective patients. So far, this service has worked well and my front-desk scheduling coordinator, a millennial, is thrilled! Birdeye® is another such option for texting and reviews. Texting can also be done through your patient management software system or even via a website management company such as Sesame Communications.

Chapter 10

AN AWAKENING

The ability to execute is more valuable than education or talent,
because it is far rarer.
—Elbert Hubbard

I describe my treatment coordination experience as an awakening. On March 30, 2018, I attended a Fortune Management Mastermind Conference in Danville, California. It was led by a former military man named Bob who had a corporate background. Bob was a no-nonsense kind of guy, direct and thought-provoking. He cast light on concerns we had about our own practices, and he challenged us to answer our own questions about how we might improve.

That day, we were introduced to a book every dentist must read, *A Message to Garcia*, by Elbert Hubbard. This treatise describes how West Point graduate, 1st Lt. Officer Andrew Summers Rowan, became famous for delivering a message deep in the jungle of Cuba. When the U.S. faced war with Spain, President William McKinley needed to supply General Calixto Garcia with military intelligence. The President asked the Officer to complete the mission. Rowan immediately replied, "Yes, sir," and was off the same day.

From Jamaica, Rowan sailed a small fishing boat across one hundred miles of open sea to Cuba. He then hacked his way through the dense vegetation to reach General Garcia. Rowan returned to the U.S. three weeks later. He was awarded a Distinguished Service Cross by the U.S. and Cuba's highest honor, the Order of Carlos Manuel de Cespedes. Rowan became a hero of the time and as popular as Buffalo Bill.

I mention Hubbard's inspirational book because the account exemplifies the qualities that we look for in our dental team members: loyalty, acting promptly without second guessing, concentrating one's energies, but most importantly, **doing what it takes to get the job done.**

Why did McKinley choose Rowan? Because he could be trusted to get the job done. The author's description of what we are looking for in a great team member, and what action we must take as leaders to get the job done really changed the way I ran my practice—forever.

WHY DOCTORS BECOME FRUSTRATED

I had been frustrated with staff not completing necessary tasks. I was most fed-up with our poor follow-through on the exam Pending and Will-Call follow-up process.

Your Pending List—patients who have not yet started treatment—represent low-hanging fruit. Your Will-all list—patients who have not yet started treatment two years after the exam—also need to be "recalled" for a follow-up exam, and also represent low-hanging fruit. The execution of this process of follow-up determines your practice success. Like Officer Rowan, your resolve to deliver a message to potential new patients must be unwavering.

I knew that my office was not the only one in the world challenged to get the treatment coordination job done well. As a result, we as business owners are burdened by repeating ourselves over and over again, week after week, month after month, asking to have tasks done to completion. When this mission is not accomplished, we get pushback. We may be told, "Don't ask," or "Don't micromanage me," or "Let's not be too pushy." Yet, you need to press on. As managers or owners, we need to review the goals until we achieve them. This is most true with patient follow-up calls. We must check on work progress, at least on a weekly basis. It takes an exceptional employee to "get the message to Garcia" without additional reminders or—heaven forbid— "micro-management."

In his book, Hubbard challenges business owners to conduct an experiment that exemplifies the problem we face. He recommends randomly asking your employees a simple question: "Could you find me the birthday of the artist Caravaggio?" What responses would *you* receive?

Would your team members say, "Who is Caravaggio?; Why do you want it?; Is this my job?; Can't you do it yourself?; Where would I find that?; Can't someone else do it?; Is that with a C or a K?; or Just Google it!" Ask yourself: How many on your team could actually get this task done? Hubbard states that as a business owner, eventually you most likely smile and say, **"I'll do it myself."**

This rang so true with what I had experienced in my own office. I pull up my own Pending and Will-Call lists that day and started calling patients myself. I decided that I would lead by example. That day, everything changed. I've been calling my own patients, myself, ever since.

What Happened Next

To my surprise, my Pending List on that date contained 907 names! Wow! I had so many new patients waiting to begin care! I started making calls. At first, I was a bit timid, but after I got through the first forty calls, it all became quite natural. Dare I say, I actually enjoyed it! Now in a rhythm, even with my active clinic schedule, I make follow-up calls each month. I can easily make forty calls during my lunch hour.

What happened next was remarkable. My patients on the Pending List, one by one, said "Yes!" to treatment. One gentleman who started Invisalign actually came for his exam nine years previously! I asked him, "What took you so long?" He replied, "No one ever called me!" After I had forwarded a copy of his initial records to his general dentist, the dental office called to thank me. This patient, a physician, hadn't seen his dentist in four years! It seems their office also had difficulty with the follow-up process!

Doctors can learn a lot about their own practice if they do the dialing. They will get to know their patients and what is going on in their lives. I now know who is getting divorced, who lost their job, who is ill, and who is taking care of elderly parents. As I build relationships with my patients, I have more empathy for their family situations. We are building relationships, and as we do, we increase the likelihood that they will be starting treatment.

During my initial follow-up audit, I soon learned that my staff was "dropping the ball." I called one woman who had come for an exam. It was now one month later and I thought that we had not heard from her. When I asked if she had given any more thought to her orthodontic treatment she replied, "Dr. Gorczyca, I wanted to come to your office. But when I phoned to ask additional questions once, and then twice, I never heard back. Even though I wanted you to be my doctor, I decided to go somewhere else."

I wanted to scream! All I could do was apologize and thank her for letting me know. I debriefed my receptionist. She had delivered the messages to the treatment coordinator, who had dropped the ball not once, but twice!

Now what happens in basketball when someone keeps "dropping the ball?" The other team gets the ball. They score points. You lose the game. The whole team loses. But, when your team reviews the score at your weekly team meeting—your treatment wins and losses—accountable people will either start "guarding the ball" or they will bench themselves. They may even quit the team. Very few responsible people want to live with the guilt of letting others down.

I tell you this true story because it may help you and your team. You may make a difficult decision that you need to bench, replace, or reassign a player. In the meantime, the doctors, as leaders, can continue to make sure that the ball is not dropped by making the new patient calls themselves.

"I HAVE A QUESTION..."

It is common for post-exam patients to call your office to ask additional questions. It is vital that your receptionist address these issues immediately. They should not default to taking a message and "passing the buck." Whoever is seated at your front desk taking patient calls must be knowledgeable and able to initiate your treatment coordination process.

I never want to hear again the words, "No one called me back"! We now have an office policy that **calls must be resolved within one business day.** The sooner the better. "If you hear it, you own it." If a team member receives a message, it must be taken care of within twenty-four hours. Phone messages can be tracked electronically but using carbon paper to document the date and reason for the call is more reliable. The receptionist can check off the carbon copy when she is sure that the treatment coordinator has taken care of the call that day. Without a reliable system in place, the dentist would have no assurance that calls are being handled to the patient's satisfaction.

Seventh Time's the Charm

Studies have shown that
80% of customers buy on the seventh attempt.
Seven is the magic number.
—Anonymous

In sales there is a saying: "Seventh time's the charm." On your first round of calls, you will make many appointments. The same is true for the second, third, and fourth rounds of calls. By the seventh round, you are most likely to have received a response from the average customer

When should you give up on following-up? Never! Keep contacting the Pending and Will-Call patients until you get a "yes" or a "no" answer.

Let's be clear. You don't want to pester people. I would call a new patient at two days, two weeks, and then call once per month. However, it is to your benefit to continue calling a prospect monthly until you get a definitive answer. Most patients will be appreciative and consider your reaching out as a sign of great customer service. It shows that you care and will value this person as a new patient. When you get a busy signal or the phone mailbox is full, you can also email, text, or send a postcard.

As you follow-up, you will learn the patient may be having other dental treatments that need to be completed. Whatever it is that is preventing them from getting started with you today, you are one step closer to "yes." You will be reminding them to put your dental treatment on their future schedule.

You may also find that some patients have moved away, which is an opportunity to update your office records. On the other hand, some patients will bring additional family members to your office for a new exam just because they received a phone call from your office.

It is by doing this phone follow-up process yourself that you truly realize that the phone is the lifeblood of your practice. I urge you to decide today, perhaps for the very first time, to take action!

YOUR TREATMENT COORDINATION SCHEDULE

> *If you are doing everything differently each time you do it,*
> *if everyone in your company is doing it by their own discretion,*
> *by their own choice rather than creating order,*
> *you're creating chaos.*
> —Michael E. Gerber

Create a consistent schedule of follow-up. Schedule an "hour of power" each day to make calls to new prospects. Set aside at least sixty minutes during every workday, undisturbed, for you or your treatment coordinator to call patients from a location where there will be no disturbances. The doctor/owner might tackle the call list after the clinic day. The treatment coordinator might choose 11:00 a.m. until noon.

Hot calls can be made within the first two days after the first encounter with the new patient while the fire is still burning. A second warm call can be made at two and four weeks. Cool calls are then made once a month. The exam date is printed on the pending and Will-Call lists. **Keep the latest pending and Will-Call printouts always on top of your desk**. It is a never-ending process.

TAKE RESPONSIBILITY

> *Ninety percent of selling is conviction*
> *and ten percent is persuasion.*
> —Shiv Khera

Avoid pre-judging a patient as not starting treatment. Sales failures are attributed to inadequate skill and not devoting the necessary energy and time to the process. Selling depends on your attitude, enthusiasm, motivation, strategies, and commitment to having a relationship with your new patient. Excuses should never be made for lack of success.

Positive emotions lead to new patients. Negative emotions turn them away. Always keep this concept in mind. You are helping your patients make a decision for treatment that's good for them. Use your sincere desire to serve your patients to help make this decision Do the work, put in the effort, follow the process, and you are guaranteed to see results.

AUTOMATED SYSTEMS

I am presently using an automated system for exam called SimplConsult (formerly OrthoCalc), which offers a financial slider that can be used during the exam. Once financial arrangements are chosen by the patient, the paperwork can be printed at the touch of a button. These personalized financial choices can also be emailed directly to the family for further consideration. Next-day follow-up email and text messaging is also included. Electronic messaging can be scheduled at one-day or one-week intervals post-exam, and every month thereafter to stay in touch with pending new patients as long as you have their cell phone number or e-mail.

This system has already yielded positive results. Every means of follow-up is another touchpoint of customer service. With automated programs, follow-up with future new patients is flawless. Computers never forget, or call in sick, and they also work on weekends. The patient can easily reply with the touch of a button. Such technology can only enhance success but will never replace human-to-human contact and customer service.

NON-SCHEDULED STARTS

> *The definition of closing is this:*
> *professionally using people's desire to own*
> *the benefits of your product.*
> —Tom Hopkins

Dr. Jamie Reynolds reports that non-scheduled starts have a conversion rate of 49.4%. This untapped potential is vital to your practice. Yet, I have heard orthodontists state that non-scheduled starts can have a conversion rate as low at 10%. Why is that?

To increase your non-scheduled starts and increase your conversion rate, try three things:

1. Do continuous periodic follow-up until you get a definitive "yes" or "no."
2. Avoid taking the patient off the Will-call list for several years, if ever.
3. Update patients consistently with specials, new services, or events that you are offering by mail or e-mail at least every ninety days.

Keep an active log of when and how many times you have contacted each patient. Take notes, especially with respect to future dates of intended treatment. Your results will surprise you. Patients lose track of time, and dentistry is one thing patients love to ignore. They may forget you altogether if you are not conscientiously diligent your following up.

PROCESSES

When more than one person is responsible,
no one is responsible.
—Anonymous

Each step of your treatment coordination process needs to be continuously reviewed and fine-tuned. From the scheduling of the new exam, to the office welcome, exam, records, start, treatment, finish, and patient referral, you want each step to run like a well-oiled machine.

It is best to assign one person, according to aptitude, for each step. Discuss these steps with your team. One person will be responsible for the consistency, quality, efficiency, and success of each step of that task. As the leader, if no one is assigned or completes each of these processes, then the person responsible is you!

To keep track of progress, record key numbers on a target board. Here the team can see office trends and results. Summary reports can be presented at weekly meetings or even at the morning huddle.

As you assign metrics, first ask for volunteers. This will produce more interest and personal ownership, in the spirit of "This is your mission, should you choose to accept it."

THE CONTRACT

A signed contract is the anchor of the treatment coordination process. Payment agreements are presented, accepted, and signed. The down payment is made. If you can get this accomplished on the day of the initial exam, you are well on your way to success. The doctor must also co-sign all of the additional paperwork—valid informed consent, HIPAA forms, and health history.

INITIAL RECORDS

Scheduling of initial records, which, depending on your specialty, might include photos, imaging, and study models, is best accomplished on the day of the initial exam. Remember: same-day starts guarantee a 100% conversion rate. The treatment coordinator must be prepared, ready, willing, and able to accomplish this. Otherwise, another team member must take over the initial records. Completion of this step is win-win for the entire team.

If you don't have someone in your office who can get the initial records task done, rearrange office assignments or hire someone new for the treatment coordination position. Anyone can be trained to do financial arrangements. The doctor can even do these alone, if necessary. But the initial records need to be managed by a skilled and competent team member. Otherwise, the growth of your business is being undermined by an unwilling or incapable treatment coordinator.

TREATMENT PLAN ACCEPTANCE

Following records, the treatment cannot truly begin until the patient has received and accepted the comprehensive plan. You have already presented an overview as part of the shared decision-making process. Now, by signing the final treatment plan acknowledging full understanding and acceptance, the patient can begin the services that you are offering.

IDEAL DENTAL ORDER OF TREATMENT - TRIAGE

The dental educational system recommends the following order of treatment to achieve the ideal health benefits for our patients:

1. Relief of pain, oral pathology
   a) Root canal therapy
2. Removal of disease
   a) Removal of plaque and tartar
   b) Treatment of caries
   c) Temporization
3. Treatment of periodontal disease
   a) Removal of subgingival plaque, tartar, and calculus
   b) Evaluation of bone loss
   c) Documentation of pocket depth and treatment as needed

   d) Referral to a periodontist if necessary
4. Specialty care
   a) Orthodontics
   b) Oral Surgery
5. Cosmetic and Restorative Dentistry

Whatever type of dentist you are, it is your responsibility to follow up with the patient after treatment has been completed by dental colleagues, in order to facilitate their starting treatment in your office. I recently called a patient on my Will-call list to ask if she had given any more thought to scheduling her orthodontic treatment. She said, "Why yes! I just finished my last root canal, and I'm ready to begin orthodontics." It had been four years since she came for her initial orthodontic exam!

CONCIERGE TREATMENT

As an orthodontist, I help to coordinate the ideal dental care for my patients. We orthodontists think of ourselves as general contractors of the mouth. It is not unusual for orthodontists to complete a new exam and, at the same time, send the patient for a comprehensive evaluation with a periodontist. Orthodontists look for gingival recession during the clinical exam and generalized and localized bone loss on the panoramic X-ray. We know that these findings will impact our diagnosis, comprehensive treatment plan, and perhaps even treatment mechanics. We also make referrals to oral surgeons for extraction of impacted third molars, and possible removal of over-retained baby teeth, as we know that an over-retained baby tooth can be a sign of a bigger underlying problem—such as tooth ankylosis, mechanical obstruction, or impaction of succedaneous permanent teeth. In the worst-case scenario, a succedaneous tooth could be missing.

Orthodontists also make referrals to cosmetic dental colleagues when we measure the maxillary anterior teeth width and find that lateral incisors are too small. Even if orthodontic treatment is done perfectly, the patient will still have trouble keeping interdental spaces closed when there is a maxillary anterior tooth mass deficiency. These patients benefit from Lumineers°, veneers, or composite or crown lateral incisor cosmetic build-up to provide ideal appearance of their "social six" teeth. We tell the patient at the initial exam to expect the need for cosmetic dental restoration after orthodontic treatment is done. We want no surprises.

Inform the patient as much as you can from the very beginning. Many patients may need additional coordination with other specialists. Take the time to get their input and buy-in so that ideal treatment can be provided and the patient is as prepared as possible.

Share the Responsibility

I will never forget the worst month I ever had in my orthodontic practice in thirty years. My treatment coordinator went on a two-week vacation. I had reviewed with my front desk receptionist that we would be doing the initial exam consultations together during this time. However, the substitute did not feel up to the task. So, she made an unannounced decision that she would just schedule all the new exams three weeks out after the treatment coordinator returned. Yikes! No new patients for two weeks! What a disaster! As you can imagine, this clandestine move did not go over well.

New-patient exams should not be left to one person. As the doctor, I also could have done these new exams myself without an assistant. Also, team cross-training and communication are crucial.

After this experience, I decided that I would never again leave the fate of new exams and follow-up dependent on just one person. The doctor can easily do this task, and all can fill in as treatment coordinator. There is never a reason to delay this essential function. I now have two people assigned to this process, including one who speaks Spanish. These "treatment coordinator delegates" are both registered dental assistants who can also complete records on the same day as the exam. I feel this is the best possible scenario.

What's the Big Deal?

Titles can be dangerous. They lead to oversized egos, territoriality, lack of teamwork, and doctors being "held hostage." Rigid roles such as "treatment coordinator" and "office manager" risk compartmentalizing a process. Titles are irrelevant. It's the results that count.

The treatment coordinator is essentially a scheduler who helps the doctor get the new patient started. She enters the demographic information into the computer. She takes notes during the consult. She can present the financial arrangements. Financing can also be handled by a front-desk receptionist or a financial coordinator. Somewhere, someone in the history of dentistry decided that dentists should not speak of money matters themselves. Some may view this task as "beneath" the doctor's professional standing. Others may think it is a conflict of interest.

But, having the doctor/owner efficiently present the financial options might be a time-saver if it means that the job can be successfully executed immediately. Try it in your own office and test the results. Decide which is best for you.

When I do the financing myself, it takes less than three minutes to explain the payment plan options and to onboard the patient. Next, I walk the patient up to the front desk, where my financial coordinator prints out the agreement the patient has chosen. Any of my assistants in the clinical area are capable of obtaining the records that day. Everyone is happy because we are all on our way to welcoming a new patient for treatment.

Dentists need not be held back by the lack of a treatment coordinator. Almost anyone can be trained for the treatment coordinator position of sales and finance, including the doctor. What is most important for this job is to have someone who is responsible, loves people, and is devoted to starting the new patient in treatment. Treatment coordination is sales.

SAME DAY STARTS REVISITED

Sales success comes after you stretch yourself
past your limits on a daily basis.
—Omar Periu

To win the treatment coordination race, get the confidence-building quick win. Try for at least one same day start every time that you are in the office. If you succeed even once per week, it could be an immediate boost to your practice production. Your team will start to notice this positive change. Then go for two same day starts, which will build momentum. This goal will soon become a habit. Good things happen when you take action!

Chapter 11

NUMBERS

Numbers are the language of business.
—Jack Stack

In his book, *Traction*, business consultant Gino Wickman tells the story of a pilot flying a small plane over the Atlantic Ocean. Halfway across the ocean the pilot tells his passengers: "I've got some bad news and some good news. The bad news is our gauges aren't working. We are lost. I have no idea how fast we are flying or in what direction we are headed. I'm also not sure how much fuel we have left. The good news is we are making great time!"

Without attention to numbers, dentists are flying blind in their business. Without data, you cannot gauge where you are, or how much you have produced or collected. You would have no understanding of your overhead, or even if you have made any profit whatsoever. You have no idea in which direction your office is flying.

THE NUMBERS GAME
Imagine a basketball game without a score and no time limit. Are the players motivated to put points on the board? When you know the score in your dental office, it makes the daily challenge of growing your practice clearer. It may even make it fun. It gives everyone a goal and a path to strive for success. Each team member will have a constant sense of accomplishment by seeing that what they do matters. Their actions can produce results, and as this book makes abundantly clear, help your office flourish. Numbers

101

remind people that they are on the same team and that they win or lose together. But numbers alone won't motivate people to do things they don't want to do. If people don't seek success, they are unlikely to do the work to be champions.

In his book, *"How to Master the Art of Selling,"* sales trainer Tom Hopkins defines the unmistakable traits of champions. Champions are professional, self-assured, and have pride and confidence in their work. They live and work in the present, focusing on what it takes to win. In addition, they are warm and care about what they do and with whom they interact. Champions keep a constant pursuit of knowledge which leads them to becoming even better.

Beyond the sharing of numbers, management must instill a desire to win. This is not an easy task, since it requires some underlying level of innate drive and skills. Self-esteem, self-motivation, and pride in accomplishment are essential for team members' need to believe that they can triumph. They must feel that winning is important. Be on the lookout for new hires with the "right stuff." In sales, some call this the "killer's instinct" of sales success. I call it the "winner's instinct."

Optimism Versus Reality

Emotions can cloud the brain,
but the numbers don't lie.

—Jack Stack

There is no magic wand, Santa Claus, or Tooth Fairy in business. If you seek optimal practice management systems, someone must roll up their sleeves and get to work. Your culture of performance must include reality grounded by numbers. Without data, you can always remain optimistic. You can overspend, over-hire, and have a great time doing it! It's okay to be hopeful, but don't be delusional! Such behavior will eventually catch up with you.

Open-book management means communicating via cold, hard, numbers. Software systems are not emotional. Data does not make excuses. Computer-generated reports reveal the facts. Numbers don't take sides or feel sorry for lack of effort or achievement. If you own a dental practice, consistently checking your practice metrics is part of your full-time job.

Everyone on your team needs to believe in the numbers and understand how their own contribution affects outcomes, including how they are personally affected. All staff need to act on their numbers and report their individual key performance indicator (KPI).

Don't wait for the accountant to review your numbers once a month, once a quarter, or once a year to determine your score. Do it yourself every day. Check your daily bank balance. Get your own mail. An office with total transparency can review the metrics at each weekly team meeting and work continuously toward achieving the same set of goals.

Doctors live or die by their numbers. They represent either financial success or a burden to the doctor and their entire family. This is why this aspect of practice management is so critical. Data also reflect the success or failure of practice management systems and hiring and firing decisions, as well as the teamwork and performance of the entire staff. Numbers are the hallmark of open-book management.

Numbers don't point fingers, nor do they make excuses or judgments. They don't play favorites or complain about external factors. Numbers are your friends. Numbers are fair to the people who do their jobs. They tell who is taking action and doing the work.

New Exams Scheduled

Many people fail in life,
not for lack of ability or brains or even courage,
but simply because they have never organized
their energies around a goal.
—Elbert Hubbard

Jay Geier of The Scheduling Institute, in a podcast with Howard Farran, states that there isn't much about dental practice management that can't be solved by more new patient exams. This is an interesting statement and a good place to start with our discussion of numbers. You can find this podcast at Howard Speaks Podcast #198, "Treat People Not Teeth" on YouTube.

New exams come from several places: patient referrals, public relations and marketing campaigns, and referring doctors. There are four exam metrics that need to be tracked: new patient calls, exams scheduled, exams completed, and exams converted.

1. New calls to the office

Your computer system can be set up to formally track new calls. If you sign up with a new patient call-tracking system linked to your phone number, you receive the actual number of new calls made as the result of specific campaigns. This metric will help you to calculate new calls converted into exams, new exams kept, and new exams starting treatment.

Check your data daily on your deposit report which includes new patient entries into your software system. Having several new patients entered per day is a win.

2. Scheduled Exams

Come up with a number of new exams that you would like to schedule each month. If you reach or exceed this number, celebrate! Each practice can set this goal, based on preference and financial targets. What's important is that you have a definite aim. Everyone in the practice works toward this known magic number.

Make patient calls to achieve goal success and report on the number progress at your weekly team meeting. Brainstorm ideas for getting more scheduled exams. Print out your management report to see if you have accomplished the number of scheduled exams that you are working to achieve each month.

Goals keep everyone motivated. You may have heard of "knowing your BAM number." We refer jokingly to this number as our Bare Axx Minimum. The doctors and staff need to generate this Bare Amount of Money to pay their bills. Aimee Muriel Nevins, a coach at Fortune Management, recommends keeping BAM numbers front and center. The BAM is the number of new exams needed to produce the new starts needed to produce the amount of money needed to pay all bills. This includes all office salaries, including that of the owner/doctor. Everything beyond the BAM is profit. However you conceptualize it, the fact is that we need to achieve a vital BAM baseline quota of exams and new patient starts to be profitable each month. We work very hard to get to that number even if it means working through lunch, staying late, or opening another day.

Using your patient software, you should be able to print out your up-to-date report of exams scheduled each month. Compare your exams for current time periods to those in the past. This report will allow you to see trends. If you know, for example, that November is historically a slow exam month, you can plan a key promotional campaign then to increase your number. Perhaps you could send an e-mail that month to every patient on your pending Will-call list inviting them back for a re-exam. Never rest when it comes to scheduling new exams.

3. COMPLETED EXAMS

Dental offices have a tremendous capacity for new patient exams. The sky is the limit! Try to complete eight new patient exams every single day. Always accommodate potential new patients. To enhance success, endeavor to get new patients into your office the day they call, or the very next day. This strategy of providing quick access virtually eliminates the problem of failed initial exam appointments.

What often happens is the schedule gets clogged with non-exam appointments, such as emergencies, recalls, and retainer checks in the orthodontic office. The new patient exams get pushed off to a later date. The patient may be scheduled for three weeks out from when contact was initially made. During this period of delay, the prospect may decide to go somewhere else for their dental care, where they can be seen earlier, or they may simply lose interest in getting treatment done at all. The longer that potential patient waits for the initial exam, the more likely it is that they will cancel. This is why the new patient visit needs to be given top priority.

4. NEW PATIENT STARTS

Doctors do a good job tracking and being intimately familiar with their exam conversion rate, which is available in most computer software systems. This metric is the second foundation of the financial success of your practice, and it deserves in-depth examination and discussion.

CONVERSION RATES

> *Twenty percent of customers take*
> *one year to make a purchase.*
> —Eric Baron

If you have a low conversion rate, it is most likely due to absence of influence; the "wow!" factor; likability; and/or follow-up. If your conversions rate is low, it's time to make a change.

Assuming that you provide good customer service and excellent care, the patient comes in wanting treatment. Why are they not following through? Perhaps it is an undoable payment plan. Or maybe you have not emphasized the value of this life-changing dental choice. You have not been able to get your patient to share your excitement and urgency in the value and need of the dental treatment you are offering.

Now comes the hard work of treatment coordination. You've got to pick up the phone and re-establish person-to-person contact. As caregivers to our patients, this is one of our full-time duties. The only way most people will say "yes" is if they are asked.

Apathy in this process is unacceptable. Responsibility for reaching out and determining the barriers to starting treatment must be shared by everyone on the dental team including the doctor. All team members must help increase the case acceptance conversion rate and keep score.

$$Conversion\ rate = \frac{new\ treatments\ started}{total\ new\ exams\ completed}$$

Your conversion rate each month will give you a numerical value of your office treatment coordination effectiveness. If you have a treatment coordinator, this will be her score as well. If not, it will be the doctor's score. The score also belongs to the entire dental team.

Rate your own treatment coordination success by the chart below:

Excellent Conversion Rate	81-100%
Very Good	71-80%
Good Conversion Rate	61-70%
Fair Conversion Rate	21-60%
Poor Conversion Rate	0-20%

Conversion rates can be improved. Coaches like Landy Chase or Jeff Palmer, Founder of Case Acceptance Academy, can train the doctor, treatment coordinator, and team members to be more effective with their patient verbal skills. Exams can be videotaped or recorded so that interactions and verbiage are improved. Effective scripts and sales techniques can be learned. Sales training and staff development will enhance conversion skills.

*The only way most patients will start treatment
is if you follow-up and ask.*

During the exam, it is imperative that the patient be asked if they would like to start treatment. Your chances of getting a "yes" are infinitely higher if you directly ask. If the patient did not say, "yes" and did not say, "no," but instead gave you one of the seven excuses, now comes the hard work of treatment coordination. This only becomes more difficult after the patient leaves your office.

Unless your conversion rate is excellent, you've got work to do. Pick up the phone and call your pending exam patients and Will-call patients. If you don't get them on the phone, send a card, send an e-mail, or send a text. **Do something** to keep the conversation and relationship going.

LEAD MEASURES

> *Never, never, never give up.*
> —Winston Churchill

The importance of new patient starts cannot be overstated. This number should be posted on an off-stage whiteboard daily, weekly and monthly. I personally have this number updated daily on a whiteboard calendar behind my desk. This graphic helps to foster focus, action, and accountability. When the team and doctor have a goal, posted and known by all, it serves as a daily motivation to "go the extra mile" and do what it takes for the goal to be reached

Here "*The 4 Disciplines of Execution*" by McChesney, Huling, and Covey come to mind. These four disciplines can help keep focus in your practice and provide a framework for managing new patient starts:

1. Focus on your Wildly Important Goals.
2. Act on Lead Measures.
3. Use a Compelling Scoreboard.
4. Create a Cadence of Accountability.

Your focus on the specific end goal of new patient starts will help each team member understand the clear, measurable target, as well as their role.

All staff personally affect the big picture of your practice success as documented on the scoreboard. Just as a basketball team must shoot to score a basket, your team must focus on what treatment coordination actions are critical to accomplish in order to achieve a new patient win.

The discipline of focusing on Lead Measures (things you can do **now**; exam follow-up phone calls made, postcards sent; texts sent) will help improve your Lag Measures (new patient starts). For your team to perform these Lead Measure actions, they must be emotionally engaged in the process and the outcome. **Everyone must know the score at all times** so that they know if the dental office is winning or losing. This visual display of the score ensures that people understand how success is measured, and what they must actually do.

Conversion Rates Over 100%

Conversion rates can be over 100% if you have begun more new case starts than you had exams that month. This may indicate that you really hustled in follow-through. Or this could mean "uh-oh!", we saw very few exams this month.

Missed Exams

I will never forget a patient who came to our orthodontic office by mistake, scheduled a new patient exam, and started treatment in our office that day, all due to confusion over directions to another office! Individuals routinely miss appointments for many reasons. Some may get lost. These same people, when contacted, will reschedule. To fill your office schedule, go after the low-hanging fruit. Call these missed exam patients!

Google Maps will not save you. Some new patients have a hard time finding a new location and simply give up. It is so important to provide thorough directions in advance of the first visit, and to call within seven minutes of failure to show. The new patient might be in your neighborhood, wandering, in need of directions—or maybe they forgot and just need to rebook

I had a patient who drove to San Francisco for an orthognathic surgical consultation. The oral surgeon's office asked him to stop at the imaging center first. My patient literally could not find the Department of Radiology, and he missed his entire appointment after driving more than one hour to get there!

Have clear and concise directions to your office on your mobile webpage and as a front desk tool for easy reference. Be clear with your directions; mention community landmarks, along with your building description and the address.

Take Action on the Missed Exams List

If you are not moving closer to what you want in sales (or in life), you probably aren't doing enough asking.
—Jack Canfield

During my treatment coordination awakening, I printed my missed exam list myself for the first time. What I found was shocking! The list had 259 names on it! I immediately started making calls to reschedule these missed opportunities! At this time, 33% of missed exam patients would reschedule no matter how long ago the exam. I would hear excuses such as "My daughter broke her leg," "We had a big game that day," or "We forgot." What matters is that these visits get rescheduled. It is always best to reschedule immediately—the same day as the missed exam. The success rate of rescheduling a recent missed exam within the same month is 50% or higher. Without attention to the missed exam list, these prospects may be lost forever.

As I write this book more than twenty-four months later, my missed exams today have fallen from 259 to 2! I personally call everyone on this list monthly and remind myself how much this is worth to my practice. Australian practice growth and marketing specialist Angus Pryor calls the missed exam list, "The gold in your practice." Take time to mine your gold. Call your missed exam list!

The Selling Process

*The sad fact is
that quantification is not being done in most businesses.
And, it's costing them a fortune!*
—Michael E. Gerber

Let's consider fifteen KPIs (key performance indicators) in the dental office selling process:

1. New patient calls answered
2. New patient exams scheduled
3. New patient exams completed
4. Exam conversion rate
5. **Calls made**
6. **Postcards sent**
7. **Texts sent**
8. **E-mails sent**
9. Records scheduled
10. Records completed
11. Records conversion rate
12. Starts scheduled
13. Starts completed
14. Same-day starts
15. Start conversion rate/mo.

Assign each of these numbers to individual team members and track them at your weekly and monthly meetings. The most important lead action items are listed in **bold**.

Never Give Up on Your Goal

*The results you achieve will be in direct proportion
to the effort you apply.*
—Denis Waitley

Years ago, I read the book, *The Millimeter Approach,* by orthodontist Donna Galante. Dr. Galante and her husband grew their start-up orthodontic practice from scratch using an incremental system of focusing on new patient exams. She never gave up on a prospect even from years back, keeping in touch on a monthly basis, and eventually getting treatment underway. Her book inspired me.

Recently at a conference, an orthodontist further coined this method as the "Until you buy or die" approach. A patient who has not said "no" to treatment is still a "yes" until you hear otherwise! Never give up!

As you do your follow-up, try to get three new patients from your lists to start care. Personally, I know that if I call one page from the Pending List—about 40 names—I can usually get one patient to schedule treatment that day. If I have time to call more than one page, I can expect increased success. This can easily be done by the doctor during the lunch hour. Save and earn money: Bring a bag lunch and make some calls!

It can be a challenge to make calls in addition to your other work as a dentist. If not at mid-day, try making calls after clinic hours or on a non-patient day. Once you have this habit, making calls will actually be fun. Yes, fun!

No one has more influence on the new patient than the doctor. My own conversion rate is high. This positive feedback loop serves as constant encouragement for me to do more. Accept that calling patients, texting, emailing, and sending postcards is a noble challenge, a rewarding experience, and the purpose of your professional life. You can't help people if you don't reach out to them. Enjoy every minute of building your new-patient relationships.

Recently, I started a new orthognathic surgery patient with braces. This young woman had come in with her family at the age of seventeen for a new patient exam **five years previously**. At that time, she was not able to afford orthodontic treatment. Now, as a twenty-two-year-old with a job and her own finances, she returned to our office. After receiving braces, she told me: "Thank you, Dr. Gorczyca. Thank you for not giving up on me." I feel very privileged to now be able to have a positive impact on her life.

Chapter 12

PLANNING

Activity breeds productivity-
you just need to be active in the right areas.
—Tom Hopkins

Plan your time. By doing so, you prevent being distracted by the next thing that grabs your attention and takes you away from your ultimate goal. For doctors, examples could include putting out fires instead of returning a call. For a treatment coordinator, this could mean an alternate task such as cleaning the closet instead of answering important new patient messages. To help you organize, write down the most important thing you must do.

Understand that **now** is the most important time. Whatever you can do to deliver new patient care **today**, do it! You will never have this moment again. Once it passes, it is gone forever. Practices that are successful get as much done as they can each day. Procrastination is not on the agenda.

THE POWER OF NOW

Don't put off until tomorrow
what you can do today.
—Benjamin Franklin

The power of today, this moment, now, is amazing. Thinking consistently, "What can I do now, for my patients?" is the mark of someone who is all-in, intentionally building a successful dental practice. "I'm busy," "tomorrow," "next week," and "next month" are the most dangerous excuse phrases that can be spoken by anyone in the office. These words are especially dangerous if spoken by a treatment coordinator. Tomorrow often never comes. By the time next month rolls around, the prospect may have lost interest in the treatment. Today is a 100% success. Don't put off scheduling the patient **today** and doing the procedure **now**. This habit guarantees success

THE PLAN

Top-notch practices have routines. They are organized. They stay focused and on track. They get the job done with grit and persistence. Nothing is left to chance. They have a plan.

Positive sales results require planning ahead. To help ensure great outcomes, here are a few common sales routines. Before you leave the office, look at the schedule for the next day and make some calls to fill in the gaps. You may do this by calling new patients who have been referred from colleagues, by emailing replies to appointment requests, or by calling recall patients who missed initial exam appointments or who are on the pending or Will-call lists. The more you reach out, the more exams and new-patient starts you will schedule.

REFERRAL CARDS

Triplicate referral cards given to referring doctors will help them easily send new patients to your office. The white copy is mailed, the yellow copy is handed to the patient, and the pink copy is kept by the referring practice. Once the white card is filled out with the patient name, phone number, and a request for a new exam, they are easily folded, stapled or taped and dropped in the mail with prepaid postage. If the patient has not yet called for an exam, you can contact them after receiving the card.

If you are a general dentist, have cards printed and given to all of your dental specialists. As an orthodontic specialist, many of our new families recently moved to the area and are looking for a family dentist. Many specialists send approximately the same number of new patients as they receive.

Keep track of the number of white cards coming in. If low, it's time for a friendly cookie run to dentists in your area to thank them, and to remind them that you appreciate their referrals.

The Routine

> *I have always found that plans are useless,*
> *but planning is indispensable.*
> —Dwight D. Eisenhower

At the end of every day, prepare your call schedule for the next day. Set everything out on your desk so you're ready to go the minute you walk through the door in the morning. If you start at 8:00 a.m., for reasons of politeness, you will need to wait an hour to make your first call. Once 9:00 a.m. hits, get rolling!

Here is an easy and effective routine you can follow:

1. Set your call list the day before.
2. Know your script. What you are going to say to a pending patient to start treatment will differ from a will-call patient who needs to come back for a re-exam. How you approach an exam no-show is not the same as an unscheduled observation or recall appointment. Don't read from your prepared text. Speak naturally but know ahead of time what you are going to say.
3. Keep track of where you are as you approach your daily, weekly, and monthly quotas. Review your goals each day with yourself and each week with the team.
4. Remind yourself of the last new patient start that you scheduled. Let it inspire you. Celebrate each success!

Talent

> *The best preparation for good work tomorrow*
> *is to do good work today.*
> —Elbert Hubbard

Great salespeople share certain characteristics. These include planning to win, expecting to succeed, eliminating barriers for success, and having persistence, grit, and confidence. Before you tear down walls for your patients, you must first get rid of your own personal impediments—whatever is holding you back from treatment coordination success—and replace them with positive attributes. These traits include:

1. Discipline
2. Focus
3. Commitment
4. Courage
5. Humility

Not everyone is cut out for sales. Evaluate your own traits and aptitudes. Do you have what it takes?

1. DISCIPLINE

> *Motivation gets you going,*
> *but discipline keeps you growing.*
> —John C. Maxwell

Whoever is in charge of new patient starts needs to report the exam numbers, the new patient starts, and the conversion rate to the doctor and the team. They must be committed to the process. These are the most important Key Performance Indicators (KPIs) for the success of the practice. Future monies will not be collected if you have no new patients. Therefore, the treatment coordination process is the cornerstone that cannot be overlooked. It needs to be given the attention that it deserves.

Your main objective is to start new patient treatment. This is your Objective Key Result (OKR). This metric should be reported at your weekly team meeting so that all are aware whether you are "on track" or "off track." If you are off track, you need to diagnose and manage more help, or to devote increased effort toward contacting the new exams you already have, or perhaps start a new marketing campaign to increase this number.

2. FOCUS

It is the most important "F" word of success: **focus**. The simple actions of knowing your goal, writing it down, and reviewing it each day, increase your chances of reaching your desired outcome. Making progress toward your end goal is your greatest motivator. Just taking the first step gets you closer to achieving it. When your focus is set, you'll know what to do.

Place a white board in your office. Write down your goals for all to see. Track your progress each day and review your results each week and month. Find fulfillment in daily progress. When the goals are visible, everyone in the process is more apt to do the work necessary to achieve the result.

3. COMMITMENT

> *The days people make the most progress are*
> *the days they feel most motivated and engaged.*
> —Daniel Pink

The most dangerous words that you can ever hear in your office are, "I think that I'll quit." The person who makes this statement is burned-out. They are out of the game. They're just looking for their final excuse to walk out the door. If you interpret these words in jest, take them seriously. Ask the employee if they would seriously like to submit their resignation at that time.

Heaven forbid that you hear the utterance, "I don't care." Such a person may actually stay and not care about your patients! These words can never be taken back. The team member who doesn't care is on the "leaving soon" list. They already have one foot out the door.

Make it easy for them. Their activities in your office are "just a job." They are not committed to the vision, the patients, their teammates, the practice, or the boss. They do not find purpose in their work. It is not inappropriate when you hear these words, to ask this team member to put their resignation in writing.

A final action that speaks even louder than these undesirable words is absenteeism. Being absent is an active choice. It marks zero input producing zero output. They don't care! Absenteeism is a big, red flag demonstrating lack of commitment. It is better to have no one than someone you can't count on to even show up. Absenteeism is the number one cause of termination.

Eliminate these unwanted behaviors forever! There is someone else in your community who would love to work in your office. All you need to do is place the job listing to find them.

4. COURAGE

> *Conflict cannot survive*
> *without your participation.*
> —Wayne Dyer

Courage overcomes fear. As the doctor/owner, and/or a treatment coordinator, you will need this attribute to face daily disappointment and from the people who say "No" to treatment

Accept the fact that the new patient you call may say, "No." Trepidation may be hindering you from reaching out. You mustn't take this feeling personally. Just say, "Thank you for letting me know." Learn from the experience, make any needed office changes, and move on

If the answer is "No," have courage to ask "Why?" I once had a patient's mother tell me that, "Your office isn't a fit." I asked, "In what way?" She replied, "The other office is $500 less expensive and our finances are really tight." I asked, "What was $500 less, the down payment or the overall treatment fee?" She explained, "The down payment." I told her, "If that is the only reason, let's lower your down payment and get you started today." She exclaimed: "Oh, that would be great! We really wanted to come to your office!" She started treatment.

Whoever does the patient follow-up phone calls must ask questions until they get the truth as to why the patient did not choose you. Whatever the reason, don't get defensive. Try to fix the issue that is blocking the patient from coming onboard. Come up with a solution to the objection. Get to "yes!"

5. HUMILITY

> *We do not learn from experience,*
> *we learn from reflecting on experience.*
> —John Dewey

As the doctor, you may be thinking: "I don't need to work on my treatment coordination success. I don't get paid to do that. I went to dental school." Be assured, everyone in the dental office needs to be part of the treatment coordination team. All hands on deck. Accept your numbers as your reality. Take your ego out of it.

Jeff Palmer of the Case Acceptance Academy states that doctors who are involved with the treatment coordination process perform better clinically than those who stay away from practice management. Dentists who are enthusiastic about treatment coordination are more successful at new patient case conversion. It behooves every practice owner to be "hands-on" when it comes to initial exam follow-up.

When you review your numbers with your team, give yourself a score:

7-10	Green	We delivered
4-6	Yellow	We made progress
1-3	Red	We can do better

Keep track of your individual team members' performance and have them report on it every week. No excuses. Just accountability and action.

SMART Goals

> *Output always equals input.*
> —James Van Fleet

In her book, *Dental Survival Guide,* Mary Beth Bajornas provides an outline that can be used for SMART goals: Specific, Measurable, Achievable, Relevant, and Time-based. This template is a useful guide and a reminder for each team member to log and track their individual monthly tasks. On a regular basis, these goals can be achieved, reported, and repeated.

When you know your numbers, actions can be taken to make things happen, especially during slow times, when you can pull out all the stops with office campaigns.

As an example, in anticipation of Mother's Day, we sent out a mass e-mail in early May to everyone in our database via the Sesame Communications link to our Ortho2 software. It stated, "Come in for an orthodontic exam before Mother's Day and receive free in-office teeth whitening." Remember, "free" is the most powerful word in marketing. It was a fun, limited-time-only offer. From this one electronic blast, we completed four new patient exams and whitening, with the end result of two new Invisalign® cases starting treatment.

Try promotion of a "use it or lose it" campaign for using dental insurance by the end of the year. Rev up your treatment coordination calls, postcards, texts, and e-mail campaigns in November and December with this message. Plan ahead.

Celebrate Success

> *A business that looks orderly says to your customer*
> *that he can trust in the result delivered.*
> —Michael E. Gerber

When you hit your goals, celebrate! Take a breath to savor your progress. Throw a party with the team. Celebrate your growing achievements. You've worked hard! Take time to enjoy the moment.

Part Three

DELIVERY

*A leader's job is to look into the future and see the organization,
not as it is, but as it should be.*

—Jack Welch

The last aspect of the treatment coordination process is delivery of the services that you have agreed to provide for the price that you have set. Here is where the make-or-break moment resides: in the follow-through. You are a partner in your patient's care. Your goals are to deliver clinical excellence, outstanding customer service, and a great patient experience. The patient's responsibility in this process is to cooperate in treatment, to pay for your services, and to refer more patients. When this happens seamlessly, it's a win-win. Congratulations! You have achieved success.

There are many steps along the path of treatment coordination. Things don't always go as planned. Now, it is your job to determine where your systems can be improved and come up with solutions.

Chapter 13

PERFORMANCE

That which is measured improves.
That which is measured and reported improves exponentially.
—Karl Pearson

No matter how much is delegated, the doctor as leader will still need to keep up on key strategic initiatives. Weekly check-ins are a management must. Take time to verify. **Never assume that important tasks are being completed without verification.**

Oversight can take place consistently at the weekly team meeting with reports distributed to all attendees. Results need to be evaluated, progress assessed, and overall performance made known to all. This exercise gives each team member incredible motivation to complete the assigned tasks and take pride in the work that they have accomplished. You may even consider giving a weekly achievement award to highlight projects completed in an exemplary fashion.

Treatment coordination operations will need to be systemized and assigned to individuals who may be capable of getting the job done, but not necessarily by nature. They may not be self-starters. You will find yourself giving constant guidance, training, and reminders. It is your job as an employer or manager to maintain productivity. It is also your duty to determine if each team member is trainable to deliver the performance you need to keep your office running smoothly.

Outcomes and performance can be easily tracked by a review of reports. Numbers reveal results; your team members can present their own work and progress at weekly meetings. The objective is to formulate a transparent and consistent format for listing, reviewing, and improving key metrics.

Present Your Results

Meetings are the moment of truth for accountability.
—Gino Wickman

Imagine a school with no tests. Do you think anyone would study? Your weekly team meeting is your in-office test of what each individual accomplished during the previous week. Presentations keep everyone accountable. Team members benefit from the ability to present their results to develop satisfaction and pride in their work. This gives everyone the opportunity to say, "Thank you" or "Well done," or "It's great having you as part of our team."

What gets rewarded gets repeated. You may want to give a monetary incentive in the form of a gift card with a thank you card for the outstanding achievement of the week. It is important to take time to show appreciation for a job well done.

Team meetings are a time to set new goals and action plans for the week ahead. After you go around the room once with report presentations, circle back a second time to ask what each team member plans to accomplish in the week ahead. These sessions enable regular feedback which can be one of the most effective tools available for achieving maximum results.

Required Doctor Performance

During the welcome orientation of the new patient, the patient or legal guardian and dentist will need to sign several documents. These include:

1. Diagnosis and Treatment Plan
2. Patient Contract
3. Informed Consent
4. Financial Contract
5. HIPAA Forms
6. Health History

In addition, the dentist will need to review the chart entries at each and every appointment. Even if the dental assistant records the treatment progress, **the dentist always needs to co-sign the visit notes.**

DELEGATE

The doctor alone cannot possibly do every job in the office. Even if they could, it would not be a very good use of their time. Dentists need to be able to rely on their team. It is our challenge to assemble performance-oriented leaders to complete jobs that need to be done. Ideally, it would be wonderful if the doctor could focus solely on those tasks that require a dental license.

In order to achieve effective delegation, assign your KPIs or OKRs to your staff. Associate a numerical target with each of these indices. Occasionally, when performance is lacking, you may need "off-site" help from a consultant to review reports with your team members. This accountable delegation will keep your office moving forward with improvement.

AUDIT

> *Vision without traction*
> *is hallucination.*
> —Gino Wickman

Years ago, I had a team member leave my office. I was concerned about her behavior, so I hired Prosperident, a dental fraud and investigation company, to perform an audit. Even though I had reviewed reports on a monthly basis, they found that many of my insurance claims were ninety days overdue. I then hired Jackie Shoemaker of Shoemaker Consulting to train my new insurance person how to bill insurance promptly, weekly, and consistently. We brought in a consultant who found that our new computer software had been set up improperly: the top line of the insurance claim form was being left blank. This one fault was causing many of our insurance claims to be rejected!

Optimizing a neglected report may take up to one year. It will require constant attention, time, and focus. With the help of an in-office consultant, we cleaned up our insurance report. Within one year, the 30+ day overdue total went from $54,000 to less than $1,500. Now, two years later, with a change of two personnel, we are in a daily insurance billing groove with less than \$1,000 past due insurance. Our system of excellence includes EOBs, same day billing, and insurance company follow-up. But this took work and change to achieve. Now, I actually have a feeling of joy whenever I sign my prepared insurance forms each day.

REPORTS

> *In God we trust; all others must bring data.*
> —W. Edwards Deming

Just like a report card with subject grades A through F, as office owner or manager, it will be your job to regularly review performance. Statistical data will help you to determine if each team member is fulfilling the tasks, or KPIs, that they were hired to do.

If you need help determining if your office reports are favorable or unfavorable, attend the management meeting of your office software company. Their experts will be able to walk you through interpretation of your management reports. You will also able to hire these experts, consultants, and coaches to improve these reports with you and your team. Focusing on improving KPIs on a weekly basis will keep your office in order and help ensure that job functions such as collecting payments, billing insurance, and calling unscheduled patients are being done effectively. Critical reports include:

- Accounts Receivable
- Insurance Aging
- Active Patients without Appointments
- Active Patients Over Treatment Time
- Pending List
- Will-Call List
- Missed Exams List
- Growth/Observation Recall without appointments
- Production
- Collections
- Payroll Overtime

Improving prioritized reports vital to your practice will help to the overall financial health of your office.

FEEDBACK

Communication in the form of feedback is a useful tool for addressing performance gaps as well as recognizing exemplary work. There are two types of feedback: (1) positive feedback offering praise; and (2) constructive feedback detailing areas for improvement.

POSITIVE FEEDBACK

Great news enhances confidence and increases a staff person's sense of commitment. It highlights what an employee does well. Reward what you value. Team members will look up to those who are praised publicly and incentivized. They will aspire to produce the same achievement results.

Positive feedback is especially helpful for recently hired personnel and those trying to master new tasks. But don't assume that your top performers and career veterans know how well they are doing or how much they are appreciated for their efforts. Tell them. Everyone needs reinforcement. The doctor also needs affirmation from time to time. Whether it comes from within the office, a patient, a coach, or even from a spouse or friend, a simple pat on the back is appreciated and feeds the soul.

CONSTRUCTIVE FEEDBACK

Praise in public, criticize in private.
—Vince Lombardi

If you are like most doctors or managers, addressing employee problems and lack of performance is among the least enjoyable aspects of owning or running a dental office. No one likes to tell a team member that their efforts are falling short of what is acceptable. But if you avoid relaying the news that their work is unsatisfactory, this pattern will continue or possibly worsen. Your disappointment will fester and may grow to a point at which this person can no longer remain. Hopefully, taking action will result in new habits producing desired outcomes.

Clear coaching helps team members understand what areas need improvement. Since your aim is to enhance performance and develop office talent, constructive feedback must be given. Each employee's work, or lack thereof, affects the success of the entire practice. When one person is perceived as not doing their job, it is demoralizing for all. The sooner you deal with performance issues, the better for everyone.

Without reviews, the poor performer may actually think they are doing satisfactory work. A frank discussion, together with presentation of KPIs, will clear up any misconception and give the employee an opportunity to get back on track, and perhaps save their job. When giving constructive feedback, stick to the facts. This is not about the person, it's about a job being done satisfactorily to completion. Listen to what the employee says and come up with a game plan for improvement.

Ask your team member how they can address the problem. Ask, "Does this sound feasible to you?" Reiterate and confirm what the employee has said. "So, your main issue is setting aside time to make phone calls, and now you will schedule one hour per day to complete forty calls per day, correct?" Each week thereafter, check progress.

Your employee may need an opportunity for development, education, or coaching. After the third attempt, ask yourself the realistic question, "Is this person trainable?" The most well-intentioned support won't succeed if the person is not receptive to change.

Identify what is causing the issue. Is it poor effort, lack of organization, or insufficient talent? Working together, you may find the answer. If the employee is not capable of rising to the challenge, you may need to make a change. A role may need to be reassigned to a more capable person. You may not have the right person, in the right seat, on your bus.

A PRODUCTIVE PUSH

Setting goals is the first step
in turning the invisible into the visible.
—Tony Robbins

In his book entitled, *How to Master the Art of Selling,* author and number one national sales trainer Tom Hopkins outlines seven motivators of great salespeople: money, security, recognition, acceptance, self-acceptance, love of family, and achievement. Employers can provide the first four of these factors: money, job security, public recognition, and acceptance by the team and the doctor.

The last three sales motivators are internal and cannot be given: self-acceptance, love of family, and achievement. We must seek and recognize these key contributors to success in those we hire. Hopefully, we can recruit and retain goal-oriented players who are confident in their capabilities, supported by family, and nourished by accomplishment.

This last sales motivator is the most important motivator of all: the desire to achieve. This drive must come from within. A sense of purpose is instilled. A winner's instinct is innate.

Outstanding treatment coordinators take tremendous pride in their profession and in themselves, their offices, and the services that they provide. They own their results.

When needed, asking a receptive team member to raise their performance is critical to office success. Encouragement helps with optimism and feeling more at ease with the daily challenges that employees face. Let your entire staff know you, as the business owner, are there to support them every step of the way.

As a doctor/boss/leader/manager/coach, be prepared for push-back. A team member may say, "You're too hard on me," or give a myriad of excuses. Blame may be cast in every direction. In response, emphasize high standards and provide assurance that they can get the job done.

Try saying, "I'm giving you these comments because we have high expectations and I know you can reach them." The message you are giving is, *"I know you are capable of great things if you will just put in the work."*

Giving direction and support is especially crucial in the position of treatment coordinator. But your employee will need their own grit to stick with it and see the task to completion. Work ethic and drive are an acquired skill for those eager to serve as treatment coordinator. But being willing to undertake corrective action is essential to motivating productive performance.

Be aware that you can't motivate a non-achiever who is willing to accept failure. No amount of education and opportunity will rescue them. With apathy and acceptance of getting by with minimum effort, corrective measures will be ineffectual. Not all productive pushes will be successful

PLAN TODAY

> *People begin to become successful*
> *the minute they decide to be.*
> —Harvey MacKay

Plan each day to achieve a small win. Short-term goal-setting starts with the immediate: What you do now. Ask, "What are we going to accomplish **today**?" Start with yourself!

If each day you accomplish **one thing**, each week will be good, each month will be good, each quarter will be good, and each year will be good. Three hundred sixty-five great todays make for a great year, year after year.

Chapter 14

SCHEDULING

*Never put off till tomorrow
what you can do today.*
—Benjamin Franklin

Try to make it an office policy for the new patient to always leave with a follow-up appointment. This habit costs you nothing; it is great customer service; and it is easier than reaching out at a later time to book the next visit. It is better for the patient to cancel their next appointment then for them not be scheduled at all.

TRACKING

Patients will go "missing" from your practice if they do not have future appointments. Make it someone's daily job to track and reschedule these recall patients. Run the "Active Patients No Appointment" report. How many names do you have on this list? Call them all today. It should be your goal to have as few patients on this list as possible. Adhere to an acceptable bottom-line number for active patients without follow-up.

Patients go missing in action (MIA) for many reasons. Maybe they have gotten too busy at work to take time to return. Sometimes a tragedy has occurred, such as a prolonged illness or a death in the family. Perhaps their circumstances have changed: they've lost their job or their insurance, and money is tight right now. Or perhaps they have moved. **Find out what is**

keeping your patient away. Let them know that you are looking forward to having them return to your office by making consistent "care calls."

I recently removed braces from a nineteen-year-old young man. Even though he was done with treatment and paid in full, it took him ten months to return to our office and have his braces removed! He had moved away and then started a new job and was finding it hard to come in. We also were finding it hard to get in touch with him. We ended up sending him a registered letter giving him thirty days before dismissal!

MIA patients will be a constant issue, despite your best efforts. Life happens. You must continuously grow your practice to make up for the inevitable MIA patients, some of whom will be permanently lost. Run your MIA report and review this KPI at your team meetings to keep this count as low as possible.

MISSING CONTRACTS

Get your house in order.
—Dr. Howard Farran

When you run your overdue treatment report, you may find another practice tune-up item: contracts never entered into the computer. This can also happen when a contract has been entered but an updated contract for additional treatment has not been entered. This may happen with Phase I orthodontic patients who continue directly into Phase II. This will appear as a Phase I patient who has exceeded their contract beyond the treatment time. Run the "Exceeded Treatment Time" report to catch this error.

MAXIMIZING CAPACITY

Passion + Production = Performance
—Robin Sharma

After new exams have been completed, scheduling records and the start appointment is the next step to growing your practice. Your office scheduler must have a "do it today" attitude. Now will never come again. You want to maximize what you can do at the present moment to fill today's and tomorrow's template.

Doctor Time Scheduling

Airlines make money only if their airplanes are always in the air. Free time for the dentist and team should be the exception, not the norm. If you want your office to operate at maximum production capacity, the doctor, dental assistants, and hygienists should be scheduled with a patient at all times.

The dentist is the main producer. Their scheduling needs to be prioritized and maximized. The doctor will also need direction from the team where to go next to stay on the treatment schedule. To avoid wasting time, a team member may need to come into the private office to say: "Doctor, on your feet! We have patients!". Train your team to get you off the computer, off the cell phone, and out into the clinic to see patients! Have your clinic director tell you which patient is next. A silent signal such as finger tap on the shoulder may also indicate: "Enough talking! Time to move on to the next patient!"

The second-biggest producers after the doctor are the hygienists, who also help discover additional treatments needed by the patient. The person who takes the initial records is the third contributor of clinical findings. Everyone on the team has the capacity to recommend office products and service. Such items include teeth whitening and appliances, such as sports mouthguards; night guards; and TMD splints. Lastly, everyone on the team can take time to ask if there are additional family members who may be in need of treatment.

Every day, untreated dental disease walks through your front door. Plan ahead and have an overflow chair available for same day exams. If you see someone new in your office—a patient's companion who might need your services—ask them if they would like to have a quick exam. This impromptu outreach may help someone in need and lead to same-day dentistry. Always stay eager to serve.

Don't let naysayers limit your office success. Don't allow the doctor's time to be the limiting factor. To avoid this problem, have one simple rule: the doctor should be treating patients at all times. This may not always happen, but it can be your office goal. Dentists in general are happiest when with patients. Eliminate unwanted idleness that contributes to doctor stress. Your most lightly-scheduled days can result in high production if you are nimble enough to add on additional exams and procedures. Make the most of your doctor's time in the office.

Scheduling Hygienist Time

The hygienist's one-hour appointment with their patient can have a strategic plan that provides for a specific system for efficiency, productivity, and the highest level of patient care. In the area of general dentistry, this is the life blood of your dental practice. Think of your dental hygiene service as a hub, your center of activity that must occur for your dental practice to achieve your business goals.

According to dental consultant and hygienist, Debbie Seidel-Bittke, RDH, BS, and CEO of Dental Practice Solutions, the hygiene appointment can be divided into four phases: Examination, Treatment Planning, Patient Care, and Patient Hand-Off.

Phase I. Examination

The first ten to fifteen minutes of the hygiene appointment are devoted to establishing rapport, seating and greeting the patient, and data collection. This phase includes medical history review, medication updates, and any surgeries since their last dental appointment. The oral soft tissues, tongue, palate, and pharynx can be assessed. Annually, the hygienist should complete a comprehensive periodontal exam (CPE.) Data collection includes obtaining routine radiographs and intra-oral photos.

During the CPE, a hygienist documents the patient's gingival health, including six-point pocket depths, bleeding on probing (BOP), recession, muco-gingival defects, furcation involvement, mobility, and occlusal issues. The hygienist will correlate diseases in the patient's medical history with the results of the CPE. At this time, periodontal-systemic relationships and how oral health can affect overall health can be discussed. Although they are not making any diagnosis, the hygienist can prepare full-mouth radiographs for the doctor to evaluate pathology, bone loss, and abnormal findings. Before completing the CPE, a hygienist will explain concepts of gingival health, inflammation, and infection.

It is important to perform oral cancer screening yearly. This can be done using a fluorescent light such as the OralID™ by Forward Science. This technology provides the clinician an aid to visualization of oral abnormalities, including precancerous and cancerous lesions and trauma. This assessment is not diagnostic of cancer, but rather a tool to pre-screen for abnormalities, especially those commonly found from the Human Papilloma Virus (HPV) virus.

If an abnormality is discovered, the patient should return in two-weeks for a re-check. If the lesion still exists, the specific protocols recommended by Forward Science should be followed. Consider a biopsy or a referral to an oral pathology center. These in-office screenings can be done for free or with a nominal $20 to $60 USD charge. Many insurance companies provide reimbursement for this potentially life-saving service. For more information, contact Forward Science, www.forwardscience.com, #ShineLightsSaveLives, and #KissOralCancerGoodbye. Remember, the HPVP series vaccine is now given until age 45.

Bring your patient into a partnership of discovery of their oral conditions for increased treatment acceptance. Communication and collaboration are key factors in getting your patients to be proactive with their care.

Phase II. Treatment Planning

A picture is worth a thousand words.
—Napoleon

The "tell, show" part of the hygienist's exam will explain what has been found and what the doctor will most likely "do" at a later time. Here the hygienist promotes the value of the services needed. Intraoral photos are powerful demonstration tools. Ask your patient if they see staining, old composites, broken teeth, holes in their teeth, tipped teeth, crowding, bleeding gums, and poor oral hygiene. Once observed and discussed, the hygienist has the opportunity to present solutions to the patient's needs.

Phase III. Patient Care

Now comes dental hygiene treatment ... cleaning, scaling, and polishing, which most patients love. Hygienists are critical to the doctor/owner, who now enters the room to continue management. This occurs about thirty to forty minutes into the hygiene appointment. The hygienist briefs the doctor as to their findings and what has already been discussed with the patient. The dentist then performs an exam and makes a diagnosis, before explaining the treatment(s) needed to restore ideal oral health.

It is helpful to have your patient hear the same information up to seven times for it to register in their mind. Seven is the magic number. Some people will understand the first time. Some individuals never comprehend fully. But, it is imperative that the dental team use the same words to describe oral conditions to help with acceptance of treatment. We have many opportunities, from the moment the patient is seated until hand-off at the front desk, to repeat what needs to be done. For larger cases, you may even want to schedule a second follow-up appointment to review the comprehensive treatment plan once the doctor has received the input of all specialists involved in comprehensive treatment planning.

It may be necessary to recommend that your patient see their medical primary care provider when system co-morbidities challenge their oral health. The dentist will make the final diagnosis for restorative care, non-surgical periodontal treatment, and, if appropriate, for diabetic testing under the ADA code D4346 "gingivitis."

Once the diagnosis and treatment plan are completed, the hygienist reviews the Reason to Return (R2R). To prevent the progress of oral disease, preventative hygiene and other measures are often urgent. A clearly elucidated R2R helps the patient to understand the critical "why" and "when" factors of the benefits of dental care, such that compliance with repeat scheduling is motivated and optimized.

Phase IV. Hand-off
Once the hygiene appointment is complete, the patient is "handed off" to the scheduling coordinator for future dental treatment and the next hygiene appointment. The patient should be escorted to the front desk or to the consultation room in order to continue to communicate what needs to happen next.

The hand-off builds upon the R2R process, what was completed at today's visit, what the patient's next steps are, when they need to return, how much time they need for their appointment, and why they need to return. The "why" emphasizes the need to schedule soon to eliminate the disease process and to achieve dental health. It can be reemphasized that the patient's dental care is important to both their oral and overall health. Here lies the key to success for case acceptance.

One Assistant, One Chair

The system of one assistant, one chair works well for productive and efficient workflow. Each team member is responsible for their own column of patients. The appointment starts and ends on time, and assistants prepare the patients for the doctor, letting him/her know where to go next. Each assistant is fully responsible for adhering to her own schedule.

An Overflow Chair

Your office will seldom run late if you have an overflow chair. Strive to bring patients in from the reception area to the overflow chair, if necessary, on time. Once they see that you are working with patients in the clinical area and they are to be seen next, they will be happy. If their treatment will not begin immediately, offer the patient a magazine or a cozy blanket. Your patient will be cared for, entertained, and comfy, and not feel that the appointment is "running late."

Practice Growth

Practice growth is dependent upon two things: The number of new exams and conversion rate.

New Exams x Conversion Rate % = New Patient Starts

Many dental practices focus only on the number of new exams. They invest thousands of dollars on marketing to get foot traffic through the front door. What they may be missing is the follow-up, consistency of communication, and effectiveness of case presentation to ensure start success. If customer service is not excellent, the dentist/owner may be losing patients out the back door. Once you deliver effective treatment coordination, your patients are more likely to refer their family and friends, all of whom contribute to practice growth. For patients, what may need to improve is your conversion rate and retention rates.

Retention of patients and their families can be achieved through enhancing satisfaction via outstanding customer service. Let your patient know how much you appreciate having them as a patient in your practice and give them as much attention as possible. They are important to you and you want them as patients for life.

MARKETING

Now, I want to emphasize internal marketing to your existing patients—within the treatment coordination process. It is much easier to convert a new patient who is internally referred by family members or friends already receiving treatment at your office.

Every day in the office is an internal marketing opportunity. To be effective, initiatives need to be consistently implemented with joy and enthusiasm and constantly repeated. It is not possible to thank patients enough for choosing your office, talking about your office to their family and friends, or referring to your office. A warm and sincere "thank you," starts the referral process. A small branded gift—whether it be a Refer a Friend card, keyring, or even a pen or pencil—comes in handy when your patient finally refers that new patient face-to-face and gives their friend or colleague your convenient item with your phone number inscribed.

For eighty-four internal marketing ideas, take a look at my first book *"It All Starts with Marketing: 201 Marketing Tips for a Successful Dental Practice."* Make internal marketing a team sport and make your patients your top referral source of new patients.

AVAILABILITY

> *Opportunity is missed by most people*
> *because it is dressed in overalls*
> *and looks like work.*
> —Thomas A. Edison

Last year, I added three additional workdays in June. This small change produced my best month of the year. It can be the same for you. Gain more new patients by being more available. Have the office open more days, add more hours, or perhaps more providers. The more appointment slots at convenient times, the more new patients will be scheduled.

CONVERSION RATE IMPROVEMENT

There are seven immediate ways to increase conversion rate:

1. Address the patient's primary motivation.

2. Improve verbal soft skills in the exam sales process.
3. Ask the patient to start treatment today.
4. Offer same day treatment.
5. Devote more time to new patient exam follow-up.
6. Offer affordable financing and payment plans.
7. Hire engaged team members while eliminating underperformers.

Discuss these steps with your team. Review all processes, tailoring them so as to be friendly to new patients. The next time someone doesn't start in your office, ask them why, and then make the necessary changes to improve your case conversion.

Chapter 15

PAYMENT

I'd rather choose the charity than have the charity choose me.
—Dr. William Hyman

Production without collections is charity. Everything up to this point in the book has focused on the new patient exam, and conversion to treatment. Production is your dental practice engine. But to keep your engine running, you need to focus on a crucial aspect of the treatment coordination: collecting payment. It is the fuel for keeping your business engine running.

MONEY IN

We make a living through payment and collections. Revenue comes from many sources—patients, insurance carriers, and third-party companies (e.g. CareCredit® or virtual credit cards)—and in many forms—cash, checks, credit and debit cards, and electronic fund transfer (EFTs). All of these means of payment need to be monitored and tracked to ensure correct and timely deposits into the business bank account.

As dentists, we don't live by what we produce. We earn our keep by maximizing what we keep after all bills are paid. The handling of financial services and systems is an important function of your dental practice, perhaps second only to the patient experience—the quality of care rendered.

RECEIPTS

Show me the money.
—Jerry Maguire

When it comes to collecting fees, you don't want any surprises. Prior to service, the new patient or responsible individual signs the diagnosis and treatment plan. Patient payment options are accepted and made crystal clear to the patient and family. A financial agreement contract must be signed by all parties. With or without insurance, this is the patient's monetary obligation in return for treatment rendered. Even if you do not have the estimate of benefits (EOB) or insurance verification, have the patient sign the contract for the full amount of the service, explicitly stating the gross usual and customary fee, anticipated insurance coverage amount, and courtesy reductions. If the patient is not paying the full fee, specifically narrate the reason, and the net fee. The contract needs the down payment and monthly amounts and due dates, as well as the fee schedule. Without this signed document, you are at risk of a misunderstanding regarding responsibilities. Financial disagreements can lead to adversity including negative online reviews or, even worse, not getting paid at all.

ENTERING THE FINANCIAL AGREEMENT INTO YOUR PRACTICE MANAGEMENT SOFTWARE

A verbal contract isn't worth the paper it's written on.
—Samuel Goldwyn

Once the contract has been signed by the patient or responsible party, employee number one is responsible for collecting the down payment, applying the down payment to the patient's ledger in the practice management software, giving the individual a receipt, and noting the details of the payment on the paperwork. Employee number two ensures that the gross fees, courtesies, insurance amounts, and net fees are correct. Once this process has been completed, employee number two enters the details into the practice management software. Employee number one is usually the treatment coordinator and employee number two is customarily the financial coordinator at the front desk. If there is just one financial employee, it behooves the doctor to verify all contracts and computer entries to have a system of checks and balances.

Wendy Askins, Chief Fraud Investigator for Prosperident, recommends adding the treatment fee, insurance, discounts, and payment arrangements in the "comments" or "notes" section of the practice management software. This helps the team to be more efficient if they need to refer back to the initial numbers. It also assists in uncovering any missing payments or deposits due to theft. The purpose of this two-party system is to lessen the risk of one single employee pocketing the down payment and entering the service fees into the computer at a lesser value. It also behooves the doctor to check the day sheet each evening to monitor that total contract amounts are correct.

The computerized financial agreement should be the same as the paper copy that has been signed by the patient or responsible party. Both contracts should detail the gross value of usual and customary fees for services rendered, the estimated insurance coverage, and any courtesy deductions. The down payment should be shown as the "initial payment," followed by subsequent monthly payments due. **A word of warning:** estimated insurance payment contracts may need to be manually altered to reflect the final benefit determination by the insurance company.

DAILY FINANCIAL REPORT

On the schedule, the financial coordinator will outline three possible financial action items for the day's appointments:

Green – Start
Yellow – Charge
Red – Stop: See financial coordinator, payment is overdue.

For the last category, one strategy to help ensure collection is to place an alert in the electronic chart that will pop up when the patient checks in. Ideally, these individuals would have been called the night before or sent a text/email to emphasize that the payment is due at the time of their appointment. Should the account be severely delinquent, a second appointment with the financial coordinator can automatically be generated. This alerts everyone on the team that there are financial issues that need to be resolved.

Accounts in need of a same-day payment can also be reviewed at the morning huddle. The bottom line is that payments need to be made that day or charged to insurance. In order to collect your daily payments efficiently and bill insurance promptly, take action and be organized in your collections systems.

An easy script for eliciting same day payments might sound like this: "How were things today? Do you plan to pay for today's services by cash, check, or credit card?" It's that simple. If the patient does not pay at the time of the appointment, then document the revised plan in the practice management system. Facilitate the transaction by having the patient's credit card on file. If the patient truly cannot pay, you may need to lower the installment amounts and/or extend the contract. Having a commitment is much better than hoping that the patient will come through later. Repeat to the patient or parent what they have promised. Follow up to make sure that agreements are honored.

If the modified payment arrangement deviates vastly from the previous terms, a new contract should be drawn up and signed by all parties. All details can be entered into the practice management software, and the patient's electronic ledger should reflect the updated understanding to ensure that the accounts receivable number is accurate.

"Just Bill My Insurance"

Despite your best efforts, there is no guarantee that the carrier will pay for services rendered. You bill insurance as a courtesy to your patient. Even if you receive payment from insurance, the patient most likely will have to pay a portion of their bill. You may have requested a down payment from your patient prior to starting treatment. You may have obtained a preauthorized EOB. Still, it is important for the patient to sign that they understand that they are financially responsible for full payment for their dental treatment—with or without insurance.

Be clear from the outset that the patient's payments begin even as the insurance company is being billed, and that the patient is responsible for the bill balance. It is better to underestimate the benefit; if more than expected, then the patient will receive a credit or refund. This practice prevents having to chase the patient for final payment of an unpaid insurance claim. Should there be a credit, this can be returned to the patient within one business day. For patients who want their refund immediately, have them come into the office to receive the refund check, and have them sign that they received it. Or, before mailing the check, make a copy and record the date sent. Refunds are best issued by physical check instead of electronically via credit cards. The refund check amount should be deducted from the patient's balance via an adjustment; the refund check number should be recorded in the practice management software.

Insurance receipts may not accrue as lump sums. In orthodontics, benefits are paid out over several months or years. Even payment for retainers may be split in two. Be clear with the patient that refunds will not be given until the insurance payment has been received in full and overpayment recorded on their account once treatment is completed. It is always best to bill the insurance carrier the day that the service was rendered. Many insurances will not pay if billed more than one year after treatment was provided.

CASH

Despite your best efforts to minimize cash payments, some patients will only pay with cash. These individuals may be day laborers or babysitters who are mostly paid in cash. Be mindful of these preferences. It is your duty as a practice owner to keep a daily eye on cash, verify computer entries and receipts, and personally deposit the money into the bank drop box, and confirm that the correct amount has been credited to your account.

The doctor taking funds to the bank guards against embezzlement. Another avenue of protection is for the doctor to check that the cash recorded in the practice management software matches the cash deposited in the bank. Don't allow handwritten receipts or the attitude, "I'll deposit the cash tomorrow" to prevail. **Cash is always best deposited on the same day.**

Tightly monitored management systems are perhaps the best way to prevent embezzlement. Cash is the riskiest situation. Doctor/owners need to review the practice management audit log of deleted transactions report to pinpoint cash payments that have been posted in the computer, then wiped in an attempt to remove any trace from the daily deposit sheet. The patient's ledger can be reviewed to determine the purpose of the deletion. Was it in error or in an attempt to steal the cash?

Money Orders

Money orders from the bank are similar to a paper check and can be deposited in a standard fashion or processed through the check-reading machine. For patients who bounce multiple checks, request a money order from the bank for future payments.

Checks

A check-scanning machine will facilitate immediate bank deposit. The technology also lets you know that there are adequate funds in your patient's account to cover the payment. Be sure that your patient does not write over the check numbers. This error may prevent checks from being read by the machine.

Patients who prefer to pay by check may be given payment booklets, or slips may be sent to them. Checks can be mailed to your office with this effective reminder system, making monthly invoices unnecessary unless payment is past due. Statements may be mailed, emailed, or sent by text.

Insurance Checks

Delta Dental, the largest dental insurance provider in the U.S., sends checks to dental offices once per week. Our Delta checks usually arrive on Tuesday. For a small fee, direct deposit is possible. Although convenient, direct deposit can cause confusion in the bookkeeping and the reconciliation process. If utilizing this method, make sure that you record it is an "insurance direct deposit." Insurance checks and insurance direct deposits should never be co-mingled because reconciliation of funds cannot be achieved for separate types of payment.

Each day, a team member can visit the websites of the insurance companies to download a list of direct deposit transactions in the patient's insurance ledger. The EOB can be downloaded and stored in the patient's file. The office's main operating account or a separate one can be used for insurance direct deposits. Either way, it is imperative that the practice owner ensure that the monthly reconciliation process is completed accurately. Personally, our office prefers receipt of insurance payments via snail-mailed hard-copy checks.

Aetna is now offering payment via the credit card machine. For this "virtual credit card" system, your office will receive a fax with the code number to enter into your credit card machine at a fee of 2% to 5%. If you choose to accept this type of transaction, you need to add an "insurance virtual payment" tab to your practice management system. Insurance checks and insurance virtual payments should never be co-mingled simply as "insurance payment" because reconciliation of funds cannot be achieved. Merchant service provider statements will record these virtual insurance payments. Personally, I feel that due to the trouble and the higher interchange rate, it is best to opt out of this "service" by calling your insurance companies and requesting checks. Keep abreast of your insurance carriers, be aware of payment options that they provide, and keep your practice management software up to date. The electronic ledger needs to reflect the correct payment schedule that appears in your insurance report and bank deposits.

Vigilance Against Fraud

Eternal vigilance is the price of eternal development.
—Gordon B. Hinckley

One of your financial goals must be to prevent becoming a victim of fraud. The bank you choose to handle your dental business assets must have a state-of-the-art fraud department. Be sure to rent your credit card machine from your bank. Beware of fraudulent operations that claim to offer lower transaction prices on credit card services. Scammers target dental offices to get banking information and set up electronic payments for fictitious credit card machines.

Your office may receive a call asking about your present credit card machine rates. These inquiries usually occur on Fridays when doctors are at CE. The caller promises a lower rate and asks for the practice's banking information. **Your receptionist must never give out financial data.**

All business owners must review every withdrawal and payment from their bank account. Each credit card charge must be reviewed. It is imperative to verify that charges are not being reversed on your credit card machine; all refunds should be issued by physical check, not via credit cards.

Check your business credit card and bank statements to make sure that there is only one credit card machine charge. If there are any unknown charges, make inquiries with your credit card company and/or bank. Stop unnecessary charges. You may ultimately need the help of an attorney to eliminate fraudulent claims.

An excellent source of current scams is www.fbi.gov/scams-and-safety. com Review fraud prevention measures with your employees and have an anti-fraud policy in your Team Handbook. If you need help in this area, contact Prosperident at www.prosperident.com for a fraud prevention handout that you can review with your team.

In 2018, I switched all banking services from my small hometown bank to Wells Fargo Small Business. It took nearly one year to reconnect all of my financial services including EFTs, credit card machine, the check reading machine, and online website payments. I then started getting invoices from an unknown vendor for monthly rental fees for credit card machines that I never had.

I could not get rid of the fraudulent entity. They constantly called my cell phone, office phone, and home phone, to the point of harassment. The company had a Better Business Bureau rating of F. It had already been sued by the state attorney generals of New York and Illinois and had two court cases in San Francisco. I found innumerable online complaints with stories similar to mine.

I had no choice but to take legal action. When finally pressed by my attorney to produce a contract, they produced a document with my forged signature! The fraudulent contract had self-renewed three times since 2002, and I had been making three monthly payments of $49, $59, and $69 electronically without my knowledge to this unknown entity for years!

Everyone overseeing my financial transactions—two bookkeepers, two accountants and a financial planner—failed to catch these thieves! I missed it, and the bank missed it. If I had not switched my banking to Wells Fargo Small Business, I would still be unknowingly paying these thieves unknown fees.

It is estimated that these fraudsters stole nearly $20,000 from me over sixteen years. My attorney was able to recover only $3,500 from the last three years due to the statute of limitations. But this incident represented a huge loss, added to which were the fees that I needed to pay my attorney.

The Dentists Insurance Company now offers fraud insurance. This type of insurance is a good idea in our present times. It can save you tens of thousands of dollars in unwanted legal costs and protect you from malfeasance from those who prey upon dental offices. Beware of: "My company can give you a better credit card machine transaction rate. Let's see what you're paying." Protect yourself by reviewing fraud with your dental team.

ELECTRONIC FUND TRANSFER

Why are EFTs desirable? Computers don't: make mistakes; overlook registered payments; call in sick; need to be reminded; get emotional or overwhelmed; or, take patient excuses for non-payment. EFTs are one of the most effective ways to be paid for the treatment that you have provided. For scheduled payments, EFTs are the way to go.

Due dates on the first and the fifteenth correspond to most patients; your monthly cash flow is then more predictable. Be sure not to schedule your own payroll on the same day most EFTs are being processed. EFT processing and deposit may take up to two days, especially considering weekends and holidays.

Another option is to have the patient select their own EFT date. This is fine, but the result may be a less regular cash flow. Do not allow EFT dates of the twenty-ninth, thirtieth, or thirty-first to be used, as these dates present calendar problems. Don't allow patients to continually 'request" a due date or amount change. Each alteration to the original contract will incur an extra charge from the EFT processing company.

EFTs also reduce past due accounts receivables caused by patient forgetfulness. In some cases, you may experience EFTs that are denied because of insufficient funds. The EFT system will alert you to the denial immediately; the credit should be removed from the ledger and the patient called immediately to arrange another form of payment. Each time an EFT is denied, an additional transaction fee is charged to the business. Just as in the case of bounced checks, you want to include EFT re-entry fee to cover this cost.

THIRD-PARTY PAYERS

Third-party payers are enablers for patients to get started with big ticket dental procedures. CareCredit®, Lending Club, and similar companies take a percentage or charge a fee for the transaction. Even so, third-party payers are assets and facilitators for getting care underway.

During your treatment coordination process, have third-party payer information on display and ready at your fingertips. Your team member may need to assist your patient to sign up for these convenient services. QR codes are now available for the patient to scan application information directly into their cellphone. With third-party payment, your practice will get paid in full at the start of treatment, minus a small transaction fee, while the patient need not come up with a down payment. It's a win-win!

EMBEZZLEMENT

Every component of the bank deposit, cash, checks,
credit card payments, and ACH deposits,
needs to agree with the totals in the practice management software.
—David Harris

Embezzlement hangs over the dental profession. Silent but pernicious, it is rampant. Many people are capable of this horrendous act, given the right conditions. Thus, vigilance for the signs and symptoms of embezzlement must be constant.

The strongest characteristic of an embezzler will be abnormal behavior. Wendy Askins, MBA, Certified Fraud Examiner and Supervising Fraud Investigator for Prosperident, states that there are six traits of embezzlers:

1. The embezzler may not want to take a day off of work or go on vacation.
2. The embezzler values alone time and may even want to clock in on the weekend.
3. The embezzler is territorial, and he/she may refuse to have work checked, shared, or reviewed.
4. The embezzler won't be open to cross-training.
5. The embezzler will be resistant to outside advisors and consultants, becoming defensive for no apparent reason.
6. The embezzler may stage overt acts of honesty. These activities may be frequent, in an attempt to cover real intentions and activities.

Wendy Askins states that, in many ways, the embezzler mimics your dream employee, who is always there to lend a helping hand, to pick up the slack, and ensure that the work is done correctly. The true dream team member is willing to be transparent. A dream teamer is eager to exhibit their work because they want the owner to appreciate how diligently they are working on behalf of the business. They love questions! On the other hand, an embezzler will delay answering questions, causing you to ask several times. They will not be able to provide logical answers, explanations, or records because their intent is to make money disappear!

To block embezzlement, dentists must not delegate the following monitoring tasks:

- Daily: Maintain possession of the sole key to your mailbox; retrieve and open the mail yourself.
- Daily: Print reports directly from the practice management system.
- Daily: Review and initial the day sheet (secure for three or more years).
- Monthly: Review the deleted transactions report.
- Monthly: Review the modified transactions and adjustment report.
- Monthly: Review the account receivables, excluding credit balances.

Practice owners may outsource the following embezzlement monitoring tasks:

- Monthly: Reconcile bank statements to practice management software for physical payments.
- Monthly: Reconcile merchant statements to practice management software for credit card payments.
- Monthly: Reconcile third-party statements to practice software for third party financing.

Embezzlement is hard if not impossible to prevent and, unfortunately, most business owners do not become aware of the situation until they are missing hundreds of thousands of dollars. Many practice owners are hesitant to ask too many questions, or to make their team members aware that they are reviewing reports and reconciling accounts because they are fearful some individuals will interpret their actions as being accusatory.

The habit of "trust and verify" ferrets out embezzlement, while detecting honest, human mistakes, keeping everyone at the top of their game. Being fully informed on all financial processes will help you to deter the embezzler. With proper systems in place, the embezzler is not going to want to work in your office. They will soon quit and move on to an "open purse" practice down the street.

If you need additional information regarding discovery and prevention of embezzlement, contact Wendy Askins or David Harris at Prosperident. Take the Embezzlement Risk Assessment Questionnaire at www.prosperident.com and find out if you have signs or symptoms of embezzlement.

COURTESIES

Discounts are the killer of the practice.
—Char Eash

That dirty little D word: discount. Set a limit on what you are willing to give in order to "close the sale." Be clear about this threshold with yourself, your treatment coordinator, your team, and whoever is making financial arrangements and writing up the contract. Discount policies—circumstances, amounts, and percentages—should be written down, assessed at year end, and updated as needed.

Doctors are constantly asked, "Do you have a discount?" It's like being asked, "Do you want to be paid less for doing the same amount of work for me?" Of course not! Yet, there will inevitably be some patients who need to feel that they "got a deal" and that you're doing something extra special just for them.

In our orthodontic office, the courtesy limit is $300 for procedures over $3,000. This is a family "savings" for starting the second family member in treatment at the same time or for payment in full at the start of treatment. Avoid using the word "discount" when describing this loyalty perk of "savings," "benefit," or "courtesy." These words maintain the value of your professional services. Reductions should be recorded on the patient's ledger to reflect the total worth of your services rendered as well as a reminder of your generosity.

There are individuals for which any "savings" is never enough. Such families will roam from office to office looking for the lowest price in town.

Make it easy for them. Send them directly to the cheapest place you know. Don't waste your time.

Your treatment, your expertise, and customer care come with a value. Price needs to be maintained in a fee-for-service office. You will never out-compete a discount chain. Whole Foods is more expensive than Costco for a reason—quality.

That being said, from a marketing standpoint, specials do work. An email campaign with a limited time offer and the words, "New Year Special: $300 off restorative treatment before February 1st for new patients" will certainly produce some new starts for those who need additional motivation. Even Nordstrom's has a Father's Day sale.

Chapter 16

CASH FLOW

The key to success is consistency.
—Zak Frazer

M oney is a touchy subject. We expect all of our families to hold up their end of our treatment contract and pay us on time. When we are not at the top of their financial priority list, for whatever reason, patients may find themselves thirty-one or more days overdue. At this point in the treatment coordination process, you and your team need to politely ask for and ultimately receive payment. This brings us to the collections process.

ACCOUNTS RECEIVABLE

"Will that be cash, check, or credit card today?" This is one script that whoever is at your front desk needs to be able to say with confidence and ease. One thing is for sure: if an employee is not able to ask for payment on the day of service, they should not be at your front desk. Whoever has the knack of asking for payment should be designated your collections champion, your financial coordinator.

When life's challenges come about, receiving smaller installments in good faith for a temporary period will strengthen your patient relationship and ultimately help grow your practice. Try, "When will you be able to make payment?," or "How much could you pay right now?"

Nothing makes some patients more upset than being reminded that they are past due on their payment. Tell the family that you understand how they feel. This will help neutralize negative feelings and help the patient to realize, once they accept the reality of what they owe, that they have a friend.

Financial misunderstandings can be alleviated by a courteous phone call during the 1–15 days overdue period. Follow up with a text or email. If no response is received, mail a polite letter or statement. This outreach will underscore the need for your bill to be paid and not pushed aside for "later." The wonderful thing about EFTs is that they help to eliminate the forgetful behavior of delayed payments.

Patients who are not asked for a payment will most likely not make one. I once had a patient who was almost done with his orthodontic treatment when I discovered that his contract had never been entered into the computer system. He had not made a single payment! He never brought this fact to our attention. (Did he think that the treatment was free?) Make no judgment about why patients didn't pay until you have confirmed that your financial coordinator asked for the payment. In this case, we had a lot of catching up to do.

Your number of accounts delinquent will determine the number of hours spent on collections each week. Jackie Shoemaker of J.M. Shoemaker Consulting states that the average collections workload is ten to fifteen accounts per hour. So, if you have twenty accounts overdue, your financial coordinator can expect to spend two hours per week on collection activity.

Delinquency

If payment is not made at the opportune in-office moment, the patient may easily slip to the 30+, 60+, 90+-day collections report. Review it at your huddles and weekly team meetings; its results will be entered on your office AR scorecard. If the patient returns to your office, you may be able to ask them for and collect the owed payment that day. If however, the patient knows you are going to be asking for the money, they may not show up for the appointment. The best situation is to stay on top of collections daily and not let past-due payments occur in the first place.

Andy Grover Cleveland of Dental Practice Ninjas states that the average office in the U.S. has approximately $50,000 in AR. These monies can be collected by a variety of methods. The first step is to run your business management system AR report and ask for payments that are due.

Payment Excuses

You can't deposit excuses.

—#bossbabe

How often have we heard, "The check is in the mail?" This is indeed the number one payment excuse. Some patients will give you every imaginable reason why they have not paid their balance, including, "I didn't see that there was an amount overdue on the last statement."

Whoever is at your front desk collecting money will be hearing many personal accounts of why payment has not been made. Illness, job loss, or even death may be the cause. Although sympathy will be felt and expressed, whoever is in the collections seat needs to be able to stay focused and say, "I am very sorry to hear that. Will you still be able to make payment arrangements, now or by the end of the month?" If you do not collect money due before the patient walks out of the office, your profit potential will never be fully realized. Now you are playing the collections game.

Number of Past Due Accounts

The object of collection letters is to get the money
without losing the customer.

—N. H. and S. K. Mager

Fifty percent of your collections patients most likely have the ability to pay you in a timely manner. For whatever reason—time, tasks, disorganization, or life events—payment has slipped their mind. It is your job to give them a friendly reminder.

How many individuals owe you money right now? How much do they owe you? With open-book management, those are the two numbers that you and everyone on your team should know. Do you know these metrics? At the time of this writing, I have seventeen patients who owe me $18,000.

Accounts ninety days overdue are "stiffing" their dentist. This situation is our own fault. These patients slipped through the cracks and developed the bad habit of not paying us, and we allowed it to happen.

In an orthodontic office, it is not unusual for patients to complete treatment and have retainers delivered without full payment. We expect that the patient will continue to meet their contractual obligation. They have, after all, been good customers. At the debond appointment, when braces are removed, they even sign an agreement that they are aware of their final balance, agreeing to pay the balance beyond what the insurance may cover. But, occasionally, patients "skip town" never to be seen or heard from again. They may move away or change to an unlisted phone number. Now comes the hard work of collecting payment for services delivered.

Collections Consistency

Exchange excuses for opportunities.
—Judy Kay Mausolf

Each day, week, and month, you or the financial coordinator will be printing your 30+, 60+, and 90+ AR report. Patients are aware that payment is past due because you have sent them a statement. Secondly, you have phoned, texted, emailed, and snail-mailed them again. But you still have received no reply and 30+ days have passed. What's most important is for your patient to know you're expecting and watching for their payment.

1. Collections Statements
Your practice may have EFTs set up, or you may be paid mostly by checks. Every once in a while, a patient's EFT or check will bounce. Now a phone call needs to be made and a 30+ collections statement needs to be mailed.

The first payment statement is not "Collections." It is simply that: a mailed statement. Once the payment is 30+ days past due, though, your statements have a different meaning. These courtesy statements can be made to stand out with a clearly seen bright pink sticker reading, "Friendly Reminder."

During the summer of 2018, I took a close look at my AR backlog. I printed the 30+-day overdue list and personally called each patient. Most families were happy to hear from me and paid their outstanding balance by credit card that day during the call.

One person claimed that she did not realize that her account was past due from her mailed statement. Later that month, she brought her statement in to show it to me. She had overlooked the word "Overdue." That day I added a new collections technique: the "Your Payment is Past Due" pink sticker.

Magic Pink Stickers

It's pretty hard to miss that you owe money when your statement comes with a large fluorescent hot pink sticker. This eye-catching tool is available from Smart Practice, at info@smartpractice.com. The 30+-days past due "Friendly Reminder" is an excellent first sticker. The pink "Your Account is 60 Days Past Due" can come next. After that, consider crossing out the "60 Days" and adding the number of days past due in ink each time you send the statement and sign your name. There is no way a patient can see this message and remain unaware that they have an overdue balance. I assure you; the statement, sticker, and doctor signature method of collections is highly effective!

One sticker I would never send is, "This Will Be Your Final Notice." A sticker reading "This Will NOT Be Your Final Notice" would probably be more effective. There's no escaping payment due. Patients can't give the service back. You will find that, if you are persistent, within the first year, 97–99% of your loyal patients will pay you. It's that last 1–3% which you may finally turn over to a collection agency.

The King of Collections

A royal means of collections is to mail your hard copy statement more than once. Minuteman Press of Concord, California, sends mailed statements every single week until payment is made. Let me tell you, this is highly effective. It inspires urgency to make a payment just to avoid getting another statement in the mail! Do not be afraid to mail unpaid invoices again and consider the fluorescent sticker alerts. Statements can also be emailed via your office management software system. This strategy is an instantaneous and no-cost way to remind your patient that payment is due.

2. Collection Phone Calls

Your "Queen of Collections" actually needs to *enjoy* the challenge of collecting money. Dialing for dollars demands a personal touch. She needs to make it her daily goal to get the past due accounts down to the lowest number possible. This metric will be reported at your team meeting. This team leader can take pride in their work and in having the smallest collection list possible.

Consider collections a marketing opportunity. It allows the financial coordinator to find out what is going on in their patient's life. Planning ahead helps to make the calls effective. Know the balance owed. Be prepared for readily available excuses. A pleasant and friendly tone wins the day—the tone should never be annoyed or mean. State the facts and the amount owed repeatedly. Have the patient commit to a date when they will make the payment before the call is concluded. The patient must understand that you are expecting to receive their payment.

You and your patient are now in this together. Make it easy for them to follow through. Order your conversation with a definite plan. Your review can include: the amount owed, the date it will be paid, your expectations, their promise to pay, the consequences of not paying, the urgency of the matter, and your follow-up plans. Always finish by telling the patient how much you appreciate their business and their payment.

If the collections person needs help, the account can become a team effort. As the doctor, I have found that when I simply call patients who have not paid in several months, leaving the message: "Please call Lyndsay at the office. Thank you for your attention to this matter," this usually prompts immediate payment that my front desk may not have been able to generate.

If you have let your collections "slip" and have a large number of patients on your list, schedule a phone-a-thon. I did this once when a financial coordinator had slowed down and eventually quit. We divided up the accounts receivable list among three team members and set up a collections session. We were soon back to a low number of people owing.

At a minimum, follow-up can be done once per week. Schedule telephoning at different times on different days to reach as many people as possible. You may want to set up a collections call schedule—e.g., the 1st, 5th, 10th, 15th, 20th, and 25th days of the month. You want to do everything possible to make it easy for your patient to pay you, avoid incurring a collections fee, and prevent being added to the 60+ or 90+ days overdue list. Once your patient enters the 60+ list, it is time to consider more formal collection procedures.

COLLECTION PHRASES

> *Ask for what you want*
> *and be prepared to get it.*
> —Maya Angelou

No need to be at a loss for words when you call to ask for payment. If you get a recording, there is not much more that you can say other than: "Please give our office a call at your earliest convenience. We look forward to hearing from you soon. Thank you for your attention to this matter."

When you reach the responsible adult who signed the contract and explain that the reason for your call is to arrange for payment, here are six collection phrases that you can use:

a) Would you be able to use your credit card now, over the phone, to bring your account up-to-date?

b) Could you mail us your outstanding balance today, or by the end of the week or month?

c) How can we work together to get your account up-to-date?

d) Please send us at least a partial installment.

e) You have not made a payment since [date]. When do you plan to pay us in full for our services?

f) Your account is seriously delinquent. If we do not receive your payment by the end of the month, we have no choice but to send your bill to a collection agency.

THE QUEEN OF COLLECTIONS

"It's that time again!" So says The Queen of Collections, Rhonda at R-Computer in Concord, California. Rhonda is the best collections coordinator that I have ever known. Should an R-computer invoice be one minute overdue, you are guaranteed to receive a friendly phone reminder from Rhonda. She is upbeat but direct, and all of her customers love her. Dare I say that hearing from Rhonda is actually a pleasant experience?

When I last spoke to Rhonda, I asked her how many clients she had to call on her accounts receivable list. She happily answered, "Five. But now I only have four!" Rhonda is on top of her game. She loves her work and it shows. She does it with efficiency and pride. No account escapes her collections excellence. I admire her abilities and dedication.

New Financial Arrangements

It's possible that due to difficult circumstances, your patient cannot get caught up on their bill. You may need to rewrite the patient's contract. When this occurs, you have two options: extend the contract length or decrease the monthly amount.

Tell the patient that you are willing to rewrite the contract once. Although less than ideal, be thankful for this compromise that provides your patient with the ability and willingness to meet their financial obligations.

3. Collection Letters

You've sent statements, you've made phone calls. All of your past-due reminders have failed. Now is the time to appeal to your patient's reasoning skills. This is serious.

Collection letters serve as a notice. Signed by the doctor, each note is written as though it is the last one. The tone must be optimistic, appreciative, and confident. Each letter states the amount due and includes the statement, "If payment has already been sent, this letter can be ignored." Your collection letters start with a friendly note and then escalate towards a crescendo of increased urgency. Your final, seventh letter states that the patient's bill will be sent to a collection agency.

In general, once 90+ days have been reached, your collection letters should be sent ten days apart. Make sure that your letters don't have typographical errors. Always keep a copy of your standard, personalized letters in the patient's file for legal documentation.

LETTER NO. 1: A FRIENDLY REMINDER

Dear John,

We are sending you a friendly reminder that your account is 30+ days past due in the amount of $106.87.

Please forward your payment today in the amount of $106.87 in order to avoid an additional late fee of $25 on your account.

Thank you very much for your cooperation in paying the balance due. We look forward to hearing from you and to seeing you again soon.

Sincerely,

Note that the patient has been made aware of the $25 late fee policy. This understanding is included in the contract the patient signed at the start of treatment.

LETTER NO. 2: WE ARE CONCERNED.

Dear Heather,

Perhaps it has escaped your attention that your account is 60+ days past due. We are concerned that you have not responded to our numerous statements and phone calls. Please let us hear from you within 30 days so that payment arrangements can be made.

Thank you for your attention to this matter.

Sincerely,

LETTER NO. 3: THERE MAY BE A PROBLEM.

Dear Sam,

Your account at our office is 90+ days past due. As one of our longtime patients, we assume that this has been a simple oversight.

Please send us at least a partial payment of your balance of $____. We are willing to make reasonable payment arrangements with you to reduce your balance.

We value you as a patient, and we would like to continue rendering care to you and your family. Please contact us within the next 10 days so that we can come up with a mutually satisfactory solution to your outstanding balance.

Sincerely,

LETTER NO. 4: THERE IS A PROBLEM.

Dear Gertrude,

Despite our frequent notices, your account is still 90+ days past due. It is now delinquent. Please call our office in the next 10 days so that we can suggest a payment plan solution. It is urgent that you contact our office as soon as possible so that you can clear your account.

Sincerely,

LETTER NO. 5: THIS IS NOT GOOD.

Dear Frank,

We have alerted you several times that your account has a 90+ days past-due balance. There has been no activity on your account since [date]. It is important that we resolve this matter as soon as possible.

Please call us this week concerning your plans for repayment in order to maintain your credit rating in our office. Please contact us immediately at 925-757-9000 so that we can make payment arrangements. Thank you.

Sincerely,

LETTER NO. 6: THIS IS UNACCEPTABLE.

Dear Sally,

Despite our numerous notices, you have not responded to our requests for payment for the dental services rendered to you. Your account is now seriously delinquent. To avoid additional late fee expenses, and additional consequences, please mail, call, or deliver your payment to our office at this time.

We must hear from you within the next 10 days in order for your account not to be sent to a collection agency. Please call us so that the delinquent status of your account can be resolved with an easy payment plan.

Sincerely,

LETTER NO. 7:. WE'VE HAD IT! YOU'RE GOING TO COLLECTIONS. CERTIFIED LETTER.

Dear Darius,

Your account is seriously past due. We have had no response to our frequent reminders. We are obliged now to consider recovering the past-due amount of $549.50 with the help of a collection agency.

If your financial circumstances make it impossible for you to pay the full amount at this time, please let us know so we can work out an acceptable schedule of installment payments.

We will transfer this account to a collection agency on [date].

Sincerely,

4. COLLECTIONS EMAIL

Your practice management software should enable you to email statements to past-due patients at the press of a button. This approach obviously is faster and more cost effective than snail mail. Be sure that your email goes only to the person who signed the contract. Have a standard email script ready for use. Emails are federally regulated by the Fair Debt Collections Practices Act (2010), just like calls and letters. Always maintain documentation of emails and all forms of patient communication in your computer system.

120+ DAYS: TIME FOR THE COLLECTION AGENCY

You've called, you've asked politely and you may have even begged. At some point, you realize that your patient is not going to pay you. You've been robbed! Your patient has stolen services. It is now time to turn them over to the police (a collection agency).

When you finally decide to turn an account over to professionals, the company will now take control. Even though you may write the patient balance off of your books after waiting the desired period of time (perhaps two years), you never know what can happen. The collection agency could still recover the payment even years later!

Be aware that once a patient's bill is sent to a collection agency, there will be financial repercussions for your office. Collection agencies typically keep half of the money that they take in or charge a fee. Fifty percent is a hefty portion of your payment to be lost, so be sure that you are ready to give up on this patient before making the decision to send them to an outside firm.

Some dentists would rather lose money than send a patient's bill to a collection agency. Some dentists fear negative reviews or starting some type of legal challenge. Personally, I have never had a problem with a patient whose overdue bill was sent to an agency. In most cases, I never heard from them again. Some bills do get paid: In my experience, agencies have been able to collect from one-third of the overdue bills that I turned over to them.

Sometimes you need to bring in the big guns. Collection agencies will continue your efforts where you have failed, or when you just plain don't want to do it. You need to make a choice on whether to send your patient to a collection agency that *does not* affect their credit, or to one that *does* affect their credit. Ask the collection agency about this option when choosing collection plans.

When using a collection agency, the blame for unpleasant calls now shifts to a third party. The dental practice is no longer the aggressor. There is a willing scapegoat. After the patient completes their payment to the collection agency, you can decide if the patient can return to your office. You may decide after this experience not to extend credit again and request payment in full or outside financing for additional services.

In the present world of social media, the potential loss of good will by sending your client to a collection agency can be made public. Attorneys who specialize in dentistry state that patient backlash problems are often initiated by requests for payment. The amount owed might not be worth the potential for a negative review.

When choosing an agency, inquire if their calls are made from the U.S. or from overseas. Dental Practice Ninjas makes personalized calls from within the U.S. www.dentalpracticeninjas.com. Another U.S. service for the orthodontic industry is Jackie Shoemaker at Jackie Shoemaker Consulting, www.jmshoemaker.com. Another collections resource for dentistry is Trojan Dental Services. Find them at www.trojanonline.com. Lastly, TSI

Transworld Systems Inc. is a popular service, but calls are made from outside the U. S. Use a collection agency as a last resort when you have done everything possible to collect payment for services that you have provided.

INSURANCE

A finance coordinator who doubles as an insurance specialist can also be a marketing opportunity for your practice. Point out to your new exam patients that your office will gladly research insurance benefits, present EOBs prior to service, file the insurance claim, accept assignment of insurance benefits, and pursue delinquent accounts. Emphasize what you will do to help the patient with dental insurance.

But be realistic. You can't guarantee that insurance will pay for your patient's dental services. Even when preauthorized, your patient's insurance may be discontinued mid-treatment, or the yearly allowance used up on other services. It is important at the beginning of treatment that you explain these concepts verbally and as part of the written contract. Have your patient sign the contract to codify that they realize that any unpaid insurance portion is their financial responsibility. Have it clearly written: "We are happy to assist you in using your insurance benefits. We have no control over what the insurance company ultimately pays."

At Gorczyca Orthodontics, we have a patient letter at debond (braces off) day that indicates the remaining insurance balance still outstanding for their orthodontic treatment, and states that if left unpaid, it will be their personal responsibility. Once again, the patient or responsible party signs an agreement that they are obligated for the remaining balance.

INSURANCE RECEIVABLES

It is best for your insurance coordinator to bill the insurance the same day that dental services are rendered. If you stick consistently with this rule, your insurance billing will never be behind. To help ensure success, some management systems provide automatic form generation as part of the software.

Many patients lose their insurance during treatment. This may be due to a change of job, loss or change in insurance, or benefits being exhausted. In these cases, the patients may need to be told: "There will be no additional insurance coverage. The remainder of the balance is your responsibility."

Fortunately, there is a magic pink A/R sticker devoted to this message as well. It is available from http://SmartPractice.com. It reads: "Your insurance company has paid its share of your bill. This statement is for the amount payable directly by you." A personal phone call to the responsible party to supplement this mailed invoice is also recommended for the most personalized and best customer service possible.

CREDIT CARD PAYMENTS

Credit cards are the costliest means of revenue collection in your office. You will be charged a fee. Check your monthly bank statement to ensure that payments are going through correctly, and reconcile the balance with what has been entered into your office management software system. Credit card payments can also be made at your front desk or via your website for those last-minute payers who need to pay after hours in order to avoid a late fee before midnight on the last day of the month. Contact your webmaster to set up credit card functionality on the site. Finally, debit cards linked to a patient's bank account can also function as credit cards.

CREDIT CARD INSURANCE REIMBURSEMENTS

Some insurance companies are now issuing reimbursements via credit card numbers faxed to the office. As noted in the prior chapter, the insurance company cannot force you to take this unwise form of payment! These card brands charge a higher interchange rate to process a keyed sale versus when a card is presented at the point of sale. In addition, the insurance company is making money via this mechanism, a kickback of sorts to themselves. **Opt out of virtual credit card payments by calling the insurance company and requesting a paper check or EFT.** It may be necessary to call this insurance company every few months to repeatedly decline this "service."

PAYMENT CARD INDUSTRY (PCI) COMPLIANCE

Credit card companies such as Visa, MasterCard, and Discover have created PCIDSS, or Payment Card Industry Data Security Standards (PCI). PCI requirements need to be met by your dental office. Otherwise, you will be charged an additional non-compliance fee, perhaps $125 or more, each month for credit card processing.

The PCI compliance test is online and consists of twelve steps of security measures to help ensure consumer and merchant privacy and protection. All systems used to transmit data must be secure and team members in the office must know how to safely handle patient credit card information. Contact your bank or credit card machine issuer for more information and request that they send your credentials for PCI compliance. They will direct you to a website where you can login to complete your PCI requirements update.

Compliance with PCI standards and the Health Insurance Portability and Accountability Act (HIPAA) overlaps. The Security Rule of HIPAA recommends a penetration test of your network, while PCI requires a vulnerability scan. If your Quarterly Vulnerability Scan (QVS) passes, meaning you don't have any PCI vulnerabilities, it is likely that your network is also secure from hackers.

TOTAL RECEIPT VERIFICATION

A man of science
has learned to believe, not by faith,
but by verification.
—Thomas Huxley

Review total receipts on a daily basis when deposits are made. Verify receipt reconciliation with your bank deposits for cash, for personal and business checks, insurance payments, and EFTs. Check your monthly report and keep records according to method payment. Each revenue basket should be roughly the same, month-to-month. If you see a dramatic shift, as in a severe reduction or missing funds, it is a sign that something is wrong.

Years ago, when I was working in a group practice as the orthodontist, we had one month where the collections were extremely low. I had been keeping the log of monthly revenue on a graph at home. I immediately saw the drop and knew that something was amiss. After hours, the office manager and I pulled charts of the last twenty patients and started to review the contracts. We found that these accounts had down payment write-offs and contract amounts lowered. Without discussion, the responsible employee was immediately relieved of collecting money and reassigned as a receptionist. **Nothing was said about the accounts.** A day later, this bad apple quit.

If you have a suspicion of embezzlement, **say nothing**. Reassign the team member to a new job not handling money. See if she quits. When she does, it is not a good sign. Chances are that a week later this fraudster will be working in another dental office that never calls for a reference or ignores your conclusion that, "Under no circumstances would we ever rehire this employee."

As a business owner, it will be your duty to keep an eye on total receipts and cash flow. No one will do this with the same vigilant eye as you. Don't expect your accountant to do this vital task. Remember, this is your business; your financial success is at stake.

Accidents and unexpected events happen. There was a period when my EFTs stopped going into my practice's bank account. I knew that something was wrong, but no one could find the problem. As you can imagine, this made my practice life temporarily very difficult. A few weeks later, I recovered $25,000 after learning that the financial company had received a mistaken notice that my bank account was closed, or so they said! A few weeks later my EFT processing company started doing their own processing rather than using the previous outside vendor. Due to this incident, I decided that it was time to get a new accountant and a new bank! Perhaps I should have changed EFT processing companies as well. The bottom line is that there is no substitute for constant vigilance.

The Fair Debt Collections Practices Act (FDCPA 2010)

All of your debt actions must comply with FDCPA, HIPAA, and all federal, state, and local collection statutes. Be sure that you have the consent of the consumer when performing collections activities. Be careful not to call or leave messages at the patient's place of employment. Be conscientious about calling during business hours and aware of the number of times that you call and contact the responsible party. Your aim is to be professional and to maintain good will while receiving payment.

Chapter 17

FINANCE

To achieve financial success, you have to stay focused
every day, every week, every month, every quarter
on how transformations affect bottom-line results.
—Randy Dobbs

Financial systems are the bedrock of your practice. Yet, there are very few courses, if any, offered on dental operational finance. Similar to HR, finance is not a popular subject for dentists. For many practice owners, brushing up on finances is like pulling (their own) teeth!

We, as dentists, pay thousands of dollars to financial planners for advice. Yet, none of them come into our offices, open the mail, pay the bills, or review the day sheet. Very few dental consultants have ever even owned a dental practice. Our education in day-to-day dental practice finance is limited mostly to discussions with our accountant, dental colleagues, and our own personal experiences.

In his book, *Transformational Leadership*, Randy Dobbs states that five things are needed to realize business financial earnings growth: cost focus, operating-process discipline, technology, metrics, and the right people. In this chapter, we will explore all five.

1. Cost Focus
In his book, *Profit First*, author Mike Michalowicz states that ninety-five percent of a company's profitability is contingent on what goes on beneath

the surface (after the sales), not what happens in the sky (the sales themselves). It is when you as a business owner scratch the surface to find out what is going on "underground" that you will "find" more money and be more profitable.

Open and honest reporting of your accounts payable at your weekly team meetings will help keep expectations about the budget in line. You may want to set a monetary ceiling on new orders. Here are suggestions for what can be done:

- Record your monthly bills on a spreadsheet or in an accounting book.
- Take care of all invoices monthly, even if you must make a partial payment.
- Keep a log of what is owed, and work to eliminate accounts payable.
- Be sure that every check that you write has an invoice number written on it, matching your ordering log.
- Confirm that your payment log matches your QuickBooks® deductions.
- Account for all checks, keeping them locked in a safe place.
- Do not use signature stamps or electronic signatures; make sure that the business owner signs each check personally.
- Monitor your goal of eliminating debt and interest charges as quickly as possible.

We are now in the age of buying groups, dental association discounts, and vast competition for dental supply sales. In the orthodontic world, Dr. Maryann Kriger, founder of the SOS Group - Steps to Orthodontic Success on facebook, has created a dashboard called OrthAzone to offer orthodontists competitive pricing. This is a resource that my office implemented in 2019.

Professional associations such as the California Dental Association and the Seattle Study Club are also setting up buyer groups to negotiate best prices. Large companies offer "buying clubs." Taking time to compare prices will save your practice thousands of dollars. Make it a team sport. Once you get started, you will enjoy reducing expenses more than you enjoy spending.

Budgeting

Make a budget for the following month based on what you collected the month prior.

Your practice's percentage goals may be:

Staff salaries	20%
Facility costs	10%
Dental supplies	10%
Office costs	10%

Office costs include all of the unforeseen occurrences, such as fixing a sink, adding a lock, or hiring a shredding service. It includes office supplies: everything from paper to staples. Office costs also include your cleaning service and office maintenance.

There's a difference between revenue and earnings. Revenue is reflected by your collections. To some, collections may seem like a lot. But once accounts payable are added in, this amount of cash shrinks substantially. Earnings is your profit—your bottom line after expenses. Earnings are not always enhanced by more growth. Earnings are, however, improved by cost reduction.

Be sure that your team members know the cost of the materials used and the sum of your invoices. This way everyone, including the doctor, will be much less inclined to waste materials or give supplies or services away for free. It has been estimated by Edwina Wood of Wood Consulting that if each orthodontic assistant wasted one bracket per day worked, (e. g. due to mistaken use, loss, or failure to reuse on the same patient) multiplied by days worked, the total loss per annum would be $30,000! This is the huge cost of carelessness!

Pay Yourself First

In his book, *Profit First,* Mike Michalowicz recommends using this equation to limit expenses:

$$\text{Collections} - \text{Profit} = \text{Expenses}$$

This equation differs from traditional accounting, which allocates what is left over as profit and earnings. As the business owner, rather than taking what's left below the line on your profit and loss statement, give yourself an expected salary above the line. This is not easy to do, but it will ensure that the doctor is paid and expenses stay under control.

Above-the-line salaries are easiest planned from a tax perspective as an S corporation. When the doctor is an employee of an S corporation, taxes are paid with payroll, limiting estimated quarterly taxes and simplifying accounting. It also allows the practice to set up a 401(k) pension and profit-sharing plan for all to participate in, including the doctor.

FIXED COSTS

With budgeting for fixed costs, there are no surprises. You are in an automatic rhythm of paying these bills. BAM is the cost of doing business.

BAM can stand for several things, e.g., baseline activity monitoring, or billing and accounting management. In our office, as discussed previously, BAM (bare axx minimum) stands for money needed for fixed costs, baseline, repeating monthly bills that will not go away. You may or may not want to include staff salaries in your BAM.

An example of fixed costs BAM without salaries might include:

Rent	$3,222
Common area maintenance fee	$2,222
Credit card fees	$450
Accountant	$440
Information technology	$417
Internet provider	$347
Postage	$327
Insurance fees	$311
Gas and electric	$302
Self-storage	$287
Website maintenance	$259
Environmental services	$250
Telecommunications	$209
Malpractice insurance	$200
Banking fees	$150
Payroll fees	$75
Sterilization	$25
Total:	$9,494

Just preparing this BAM list for this book allowed me to remove three unnecessary recurring expenses that produced nothing for my practice. Look at your own list of fixed costs. Is there something you could eliminate?

At the rate of fixed costs shown above, monthly collections less than $95,000 would make these fixed costs high. One challenge is rent and common area maintenance fees. These can be renegotiated by contacting Mr. George Vaill at www.georgevaill.com.

FRIDAY MORNING FRAUD

When you are at a Friday CE, it is not unusual for your phone to ring with a fraudulent caller on the line. The scammer usually claims to represent a well-known fixed cost company. He next says that money is owed and immediate payment by credit card needs to be made or something bad will happen; lights or phone will be turned off by 1:00 p.m. that day. When you know this call is fake, you can confidently say: "I don't believe you. I've paid my bill," and listen for the hang-up! But what if your young receptionist answers the phone? She may panic. Heaven forbid she gives this fraudulent caller your credit card number and makes the payment!

Dentists are targets of fraud. Be aware that utility companies will never call your office. They would send statements, even certified mail, and you would be given plenty of notice if something ever were truly wrong. Phishers are sophisticated. They may even email or fax a statement on what looks like company stationery. Keep accurate records and educate your team to recognize fraud. For more information on preventative measures and team training, contact Prosperident at http://prosperident.com/.

2. OPERATING DISCIPLINE

Every morning I go online and check my business account balance. I share this figure with my team and make them aware of payroll, outstanding bills and recent invoices. We call this "open book management."

Leave no surprises. Team members may think that the practice and the doctor have unlimited resources. My staff has said the most ridiculous things to me when it comes to cost containment and cash flow. My mother used to say, "Money doesn't grow on trees." Your team may state they are "underpaid." They are not! They are well paid! Let them know that. Employee costs include staff salaries, overtime, paid vacations, sick days (mandatory in the state of California), 401(k) matching, uniforms, team outings, and

CE courses. Payroll is the largest expense of all. We aim to keep HR at 20%–25% of total variable costs. A team member may want to write off patient contracts. Tell her it is her own choice if she would personally like to pay this patient's bill. Let your team know that they earn their raises and opportunities through practice profitability.

GET YOUR OWN MAIL

During my thirty-year career, I searched the globe for the very best accountant I could find. When I found him, the first piece of advice he gave me was, "Get your own mail."

Here are examples of things that you will find in your mail: bills for services that have been discontinued or not ordered, unknown statements, erroneous invoices, and unnecessary charges. You'd like to think your team is on top of payments and practice management, but this may not be the case. No one will ever care about your practice as much as you do as the owner.

We want no financial surprises. There are many benefits of the doctor collecting their own mail, organizing invoices, and keeping track of accounts payable. If you can afford the luxury of hiring someone trustworthy, dependable, and well-organized to do this for you, such as an outside bookkeeper, good for you. But there may be supply invoices, refunds, or tax and insurance checks in that mail that are worth seeing.

Enthusiastic vendors visit your office weekly, putting high pressure on your team members to place large orders. Have a system in place so that your assistant in charge of supplies is getting permission from you, the owner, before placing orders. The easiest system of supply budgeting is to not exceed 10% of the collections from the previous month. You could also take the prior year's collections divided by 12—again, not to exceed 10%. Your ordering assistant is accountable for what your practice can afford.

Switch to a "just in time "(JIT) supply chain logistics mindset. Reacting to big specials results in supplies sitting on your shelf for months or even years. Large deliveries even at a "discount" severely impede your cash flow. Unused items stick you with a large, unnecessary bill. Mothballed inventory represents opportunity cost, debt service, and lost investment opportunities.

I once had an assistant who loved Costco. She placed regular orders for things she needed, sometimes on a daily basis. The problem was that Costco had a $50 minimum delivery charge. So, what happened? A giant box would arrive from Costco. Contained in the box would be paperclips, enough for the next ten years! The cost would inevitably be—you guessed it—$50 or more, whereas a $1.99 box from Office Max would have sufficed. Other giant boxes can include disinfectants, which can expire; or consumables, which can be perishable. I once had to discard an army's worth of non-dairy creamer cups which had expired. I now buy single containers of powdered creamer at Safeway.

Ideal inventory management means a minimum of two weeks and a maximum of one-month shelf time. So, when approached by a vendor selling a year's worth of product with three months free, what are financially savvy dentists going to say? "No, thank you."

Invoices

> *A pile of bills and statements—*
> *whether paid or not—is a sign that someone is clueless about*
> *what's coming in and going out.*
> —Suze Orman

Just yesterday, I received a statement from AT&T. I looked at it and said, "What's this?" The bill was for next door. What if this check had been prepared and just given to me to sign?

Invoices are littered with mistakes. Check every order delivered, matching it to the invoice and the entry date in the ordering book or spreadsheet. Keep electronic records of every invoice number paid. Charges can also be wrong. It is possible that you could be billed for items that you did not even order! Shipments could also be incomplete or might never arrive at all.

I once had a colleague who received $250 worth of dental gloves along with the invoice "Payment Due." She knew that she had not ordered these, so it was easy for her to send them back. What if she had just accepted the order and paid the invoice? This is the hoped-for result of some unethical vendors.

Once, my monthly orthodontic lab bill was uncommonly high. I checked the statement line by line: retainer $70, retainer $70.... retainer $700! One retainer was marked at ten times the normal price! Was it made of gold? The company was called and they corrected the oversight. But what if I had not caught this? That would have been a pretty big vendor Christmas bonus!

INVENTORY

> *If your practice is not controlling inventory,*
> *then your inventory is controlling you!*
> —R. Kim Bleiweiss

In a podcast interview with Dr. Howard Farran for *Dentistry Uncensored,* R. Kim Bleiweiss, MBA discussed the topic of inventory theft. Larceny targets include everything from computer ink and lightbulbs, to toothpaste and postage stamps. The point is, taken supplies can easily add up to thousands of dollars of lost income. Lean Dental Solutions™ offers a method of dental office inventory control. They can be found at www.gmmouse.com.

VARIABLE COSTS

When you are organized enough to have a low shelf-life of the products that you use, you are most profitable. So clean out your closets and drawers! In my own orthodontic practice, we have twenty-seven vendors who come under variable cost accounting. These goods and services include orthodontic equipment, handpiece repair, and lab fees. This produces 6%–10% of our "service" variable costs. Other samples include office items, printing, and patient forms. This represents another 10% of "office" variable costs.

TRUE COSTS

The True Cost of Inventory = Item Price + Opportunity Cost + Carrying Cost + Hidden Cost. Hidden costs include shipping charges. Always ask for free shipment.

There is no such thing as a free lunch. Sales reps will often want to meet with team members, without the doctor being present. There may even be staff who receive kickbacks for supplies ordered. Make sure that your favored vendors understand your office purchase policies. Team members must also understand your purchase policies. Team members may call experts asking questions. The next thing you know, you'll receive a bill for four hours of consulting! This can be prevented with the right systems in place. Once your price-setting, inventory, and vendor authorizations are organized, you can truly negotiate among vendors for the best price, reduce inventory, and have a goal of having a two- to four-week supply on hand.

COST OF GOODS SOLD

The cost of goods sold (COGS) not only includes your expensive materials, but also a fraction of your operating and labor costs, including doctor time. What's left is profit. Some dental consultants state that COGS cannot be calculated for dentistry. Why not? Growth will not fix a miscalculation of a negative cost of goods sold; growth will only make it worse! Optimally, we must consider the COGS and charge appropriately.

If you are placing bonded lingual orthodontic wires or perhaps an anterior composite that requires adhesive costing $120 per tube and twenty minutes of doctor and staff chair time, then you need to be charging at least three times the cost of the materials used in order to make a profit. Whatever your fixed costs of running your practice per hour, that hour or fraction thereof must also be factored into the equation. If you don't track costs, you may actually be **losing money** on some procedures. Underpriced procedures may give a short-term cash injection, but long-term, they lead to negative cash flow.

Dentists tend to give a lot away for free. These "free" checks require gloves, masks, bags for sterilized instruments, suction tips, and add to operating and labor costs. Need I go on? Dentists pay for these costs. Get out of the habit of providing free services! Charge at least an appointment fee for seeing a patient.

In my early years, I tended not to charge for many extra services such as long-term retainer checks, bonded lingual wires, or even a positioner. As operating costs increased, I gradually sought payment for these "small" items and patients were more than willing to pay for them. I created an "Additional Services" invoice sheet that listed these "value-added" costs. To my surprise, these small items totaled an annual revenue of $80,000 per year!

CREDIT AND LOANS

A credit card is an evil trap as they present an unnecessary cost of interest. Yet, many large dental vendors are creating their own credit card companies and urging dentists to use them. Some companies will only accept credit card payment. It is easy for the spending to get out of control with invisible credit card charges.

Review every charge on your credit card bill. Check the interest rate. At this time of my writing, the average credit card annual percentage rate (APR) in the U.S. is 17.30%. The highest I have seen is 29%! Ouch! The lowest average APR (in the low interest category) is 14.08%. These interest rates are highway robbery! Put your credit card away. Better yet, cut it in half! Use checks or bank wires whenever possible and pay off that credit card balance ASAP.

Short-term loans and business lines of credit from your bank are financing options to have in case of unforeseen emergencies. If you need an emergency fund, this is the way to go. Interest rates are often as low as 5%.

3. TECHNOLOGY

Information technology (IT) can now replace many labor-intensive functions including appointment reminders, sending invoices, and inquiring about patient start updates. Implement technology to increase office efficiency however you can.

However, beware of open-ended IT money sinks. I remember reading of a dentist who got into a service contract with a website company. Before he was done, he ended up paying $40,000 for a new website! Before contracting for any IT service, get a job estimate of price to completion. Otherwise, you will be entering into an open-ended contract, removing you from the financial driver's seat.

NEVER-ENDING UPGRADES

Computer equipment and programs are continuously being "upgraded." You could always buy new technology every year, without limit. This bad habit does nothing to grow your business. Patients will never choose your office because of your computer equipment.

As long as you can run your dental management software system, your current IT set-up is fine. If IT's not broken, don't fix IT! Local IT companies are not likely to pester you to purchase additional updates the way that national software vendors will. For repairs and maintenance, go local.

4. METRICS

> *What gets measured gets managed.*
> —Peter Drucker

Reporting your metrics will keep everyone on your team engaged. A goal of treatment coordination is to create successful financial results. Dedicate one staff meeting per month solely to review of financial measurements. A standardized office scorecard can help you track financial measures and might look like this:

Financial Scorecard
Collections
Cash balance
Accounts payable
30+ Patient accounts receivable
30+ Days insurance receivable
Inventory
Marketing proposals
Payroll
Payroll overtime
Inventory

Cash Flow

> *Never take your eyes off the cash flow,*
> *because it's the life blood of business.*
> —Richard Branson

They say sex, money, and religion are things that we dare not talk about. Take time to talk about money! Doing this with your team will make you better at managing finances. Talk with your banker. Talk with your accountant. Talk with your financial planner. Talk with your spouse about money!

The more you talk, read, think, and organize your financial life, the better you will become at managing it. Create a cash flow monthly forecast. Modelling your cash flow could go something like this. Pay fixed expenses at the beginning of the month. This would include all of your facility costs, such as rent or mortgage. Next, complete your payroll. Then pay your variable costs, usually by the tenth of the month. Then, complete your payroll again. Next, finish your variable costs, usually on the 25th. Then, get ready to start all over again!

Make the changes needed to titrate your system. This may include tightening inventory costs, reducing overtime, or decreasing the size of your team. You may need to work longer hours or shorter hours, depending on patient flow. Eliminate all wasteful spending.

In the game of open-book management, the team owns the numbers. Every person is expected and enabled to act to improve performance by keeping score. This is the information of your company. And, it is reviewed week by week, by report and repetition, over and over again, in an effort to get the forecast just right. This is common-sense business management, and it works.

5. The Right People

> *If we get the right people in the right job*
> *we've won the game.*
> —Jack Welch

Your team will be pulled together from different backgrounds into one profitable business. You need to create a "high speed culture" for the foundation of the "take action" mentality of success. You will also need to assess quickly if your new hires are trainable. Working interviews help. Still, it may take up to six months to fully realize whether a team member is an asset or a liability.

Breaking up is hard to do. Many dentists carry on in difficult situations with underperforming team members for months or even years, suffering at their own peril. Although we hire for attitude and train for skills, getting the job done is our ultimate goal. Positive energy will flow only when jobs are completed well. Each team member, including the doctor, is accountable for their results.

It is a shared responsibility to protect the practice from negativity, poor performers, and office sabotage. A wrong hire can drain the life out of your practice. A nonperforming team member may not make an effort, make costly mistakes, or drag down your organization. It is here that the phrase, "Hire slow, fire fast" comes into play.

You can't allow a single person on your team to prevent you from shooting for and achieving your practice goals. So have the courage, communication, and candor to eliminate those who don't care, don't want to, or can't handle the challenge of fully participating in a winning effort.

Your Weekly Team Meeting

We've all heard of morning huddles, that precious fifteen minutes at the start of the day when we review the day's schedule, report any special events, set a daily goal, and psyche ourselves up with a motivational high five. But what about The Great Huddle, that productive time each week when the team members present their individual and office accomplishments? Numbers don't appear from an imaginary place; they come directly from the people who either produce or don't produce them. You need everyone on your team to demonstrably own their numbers.

At your meeting, go around the room twice. Let each team member speak. First, have them report their KPI, their outcome, and what they have achieved that week or that month. Ask, "Is there anything that we can do to help you to improve your score?" Second, ask for new ideas and projects, or solutions to problems. Keep track and follow up the next week. We're in this together. We're a team.

Team Development

With good team members, team development is an investment. With team members who have difficulty with comprehension or who need to be monitored on the same task three or more times, this effort is a wasteful expense.

One area of development that warrants attention is computer training. A tech-savvy person can quickly solve almost any problem on their own, with little or no outside help. Team members who do not know how to work the office management system and cannot learn quickly can cost thousands of dollars in consultant time. Digitally-challenged employees rack up the IT bill and remind us that not everyone is trainable.

I once had two technological neophytes at my front desk at the same time. My IT consulting needs were costing nearly $900 per month; additionally, I needed to bring in consultants to review insurance billing and patient account entries. These two employees were replaced with one experienced computer-savvy front office team member. My IT costs fell to nearly $0 from the day that I hired her! Not only did she reduce employee costs, she lowered my training and computer expenses. Integrating new technology into our management system also became a breeze. It can be the same for you.

Coaching of the Doctor

Be better than you were yesterday.
—Jon Gordon

There may come a time when the doctor or office manager has a "blind spot." Something in the practice is not right but you can't figure out exactly what it is. You can't see the bump on your own back. At this time, you will need a coach.

Take advantage of coaching. Tell your team, "I need this for me to be able to lead you better." Coaching can offer strategic advantages that can save and earn time and money in the long run. Coaches can spot unknown circumstances in addition to keeping everyone highly motivated. Areas that are most benefitted by coaching include doctor leadership development.

Coaching agreements are substantial. I was once offered a thirty-month contract without any trial period or option for discontinuation; I would have been obligated to pay $75,000! I successfully renegotiated, and you can, too. Tailor all agreements to precisely suit your personal and professional needs.

Chapter 18

PROFITABILITY

In the end, all business operations can be reduced to three words: people, product, profit.

—Lee Iacocca

In his book, *Focus*, Al Ries contrasts the sun with a laser beam. The sun diffuses its billion kilowatts of energy in every direction, and the result is a sunburn. A laser, with just a few kilowatts of energy focused in a single beam, can cut through steel. This is the power of focus.

Everyone on your team must know what is important and what is the top priority. Hopefully, the treatment coordination activities mentioned in this book will become top priorities for your dental practice. A million-dollar dental practice might have only five team members. Each person needs to effectively execute the essential functions necessary to keep your practice efficient and profitable. Your team needs to be cross-trained and able to work together and willing to fill in for each other at a moment's notice. The more efficiently each team member completes his/her individual tasks, the more profitable your practice will be.

Under-performers need to be replaced, or worse yet, supplemented by an additional new hire to get the same amount of work done. If a team member cannot solve problems on his/her own, your office costs will be higher as you hire consultants. If attendance is poor, you may need to hire an additional person for a job that could be effectively done by one reliable individual. The more that you refine your systems and hold individuals accountable, the higher your team peak performance will be. The resultant happier team will better care for your patients and your practice's focus on profitability will be realized.

PRIORITIES

Urgent is the enemy of important.
　　　　　　　—Gino Wickman

As business owners, we get caught up in daily activities that take us away from the basic profitability concept. We need to be reminded that success requires that we sell a service product for a profit. We should not waste precious capital on unnecessary diversions, which we often call "being busy." Busy is the opposite of productive.

"I'm busy" may be the two most dangerous words in dental practice management. The next time that you hear someone say those words, ask them, "Busy doing what?" Aimee Muriel Nevins, coach at Fortune Management, reminds me that "Being busy is not necessarily being profitable." For example, pursuits that get you better known in the community may be great, but for each expenditure, we need to ask, "Did this business activity contribute to making a profit?"

DESTROYERS OF PROFITABILITY
Three main destroyers of profitability are difficult patients, impossible doctors, and treatment needing to be redone. Let's review each of these factors so that we can avoid these traps, eliminating them from practice life forever.

DIFFICULT PATIENTS
In my book, *At Your Service: 5-Star Customer Care for a Successful Dental Practice,* I discuss the "I'm OK, you're not OK patient" who will never be satisfied. This is the patient who goes for five opinions because all of their previous dentists were "no good." They need three or more diagnostic wax-ups before accepting cosmetic treatment, if they do at all. They will want their implants redone. They will come in once a week, every week, with or without an appointment, to have the tiniest of concerns checked.

They will want to stay in the office for hours. Then at the end of this arduous, time-consuming and difficult process, they will give you a one-star review on Yelp.

These high-maintenance patients cost thousands of dollars in time, materials, office anguish, reputation, and lost referrals. It is best to avoid these patients like the plague. They will drag you and everyone in your office down. Save yourselves while you can.

When ego predominates, it is sometimes hard for the dentist to let these patients go. We convince ourselves that we will be better than the last five dentists. We want to help everyone. And, besides, they like us!

Beware of the individual who talks excessively at the initial exam about all that is wrong with other dentists. If you accept this patient, you are next on their list! Throughout the initial exam conversation, these people will be pointing to their teeth and looking at them close-up in the mirror. Difficult patients are "exacting" to the point of unrealistic expectations and ridiculous demands. They may be obsessed with their dentition or have a dysmorphic psychological syndrome.

Consider how long the patient takes during the initial exam process. Are they agreeable? If they are asking for explanations over and over again, requesting special products, or bringing in pictures of how they want to look—you may want to charge a substantial surcharge for treatment. However, even a high fee may not discourage this patient from seeking care in your office. You may want to suggest that the individual be treated at a nearby dental school.

In the end, even if you have provided excellent customer service and care, yielding to their every need and whim, these patients may still give you a one-star online review. Are you willing to suffer the adverse consequences of treating the "I'm OK, you're not OK" patient? This is a difficult decision to make but one that you must consider for practice success and limiting liability.

Three Rules of Treating Difficult Patients

1. Have Limits

You may think that playing nice will effectively manage a difficult patient. I assure you, it will not. Difficult patients are never satisfied. Be sure you have everything documented in writing. Take frequent clinical pictures. Use the photos when you discuss treatment and address each patient concern by writing on these photos. When the patient speaks about how they "feel" about their teeth, remind the patient that you can treat teeth, but you cannot treat feelings. Ask them to draw what they are talking about on the photo. You may even want them to sign the photo to acknowledge what they see and what was discussed.

2. RAISE FEES

No matter how high you raise your fees, this may not dissuade the difficult patient. In fact, it may have the opposite effect. I once had a professor at the Harvard School of Dental Medicine who did not enjoy delivering full dentures. In his private practice, he raised his fees for dentures to be twice that of all the other area dentists. To his surprise, the demand for his prosthodontic prowess only grew. Suddenly, he was perceived as an expert in denture fabrication!

If you will be doing diagnostic wax-ups for a problematic patient, be aware they may ask for a second or third. This may be a warning sign. Charge the difficult patient for each model and for your time spent with them. After the third attempt, you may want to tell the patient, "I don't think that I can make you happy. You may want to consider seeking dental treatment somewhere else."

3. FINISH THE TREATMENT PLAN

In the end, despite your every service gesture, you will realize that you can never make the difficult patient happy. They may cause anxiety and unrest in your practice and your personal life. Once you complete treatment and they are properly discharged from your office, you and everyone on your team will breathe a sigh of relief. You will wonder how it is that you got manipulated by this troublesome person in the first place.

IMPOSSIBLE DOCTORS

As an orthodontic specialist, I have worked with more than one hundred general dentists. I can tell you from experience that there are a few impossible doctors. These dentists are so driven by an unachievable level of perfection, that they become crazy, make their patients unhappy, and drive their orthodontists, oral surgeons, and periodontists to the limit of what is doable.

I once had a general dentist for whom I was placing maxillary lateral implants. For *years* we went back and forth on a patient who was having #7 and #10 implants placed. The notes came back "Tip the root tip .25 mm to the distal" or "Open the space for #10 .25 mm more." Numerous panoramic and PA X-rays were taken. Several study models were produced. The dentist even delivered an acetate overlay of how he wanted the teeth to look on the panoramic radiograph! The case was sent for review to the Spear Institute!

Out of desperation, I showed the case to Dr. Vince Kokich Sr., the father of interdisciplinary orthodontics, to make sure that I was not missing some important detail of lateral tooth positioning. His only comment was, "Looks great to me!"

In the end, four years later, the case turned out beautifully, but there was no appreciable difference between the case at year one versus year four of orthodontic treatment. This same type of case was being treated by an AACD dentist who sent one note: "Make #7 and #10 spaces 7 mm in width and provide distal root tip for stability and ideal implant placement." This case was completed in four months. The patient and the specialist were happy. Patient satisfaction was delivered at a profit for the dentist and specialists with less heartache and inconvenience for everyone involved.

RETREATMENT

Take final records. Once your ideal plan is completed, the body and teeth will continue to change. Teeth can relapse and change after dental treatment. This is why orthodontists recommend retention for life. There exists a dental physiological phenomenon in all humans called mesial drift. If a patent never wears their retainer from the moment braces are removed, teeth are guaranteed to move.

In dentistry, teeth may need root canals or retreatment. Gums may recede over time, making some restorations appear unaesthetic. When there is a problem, retreatment at no charge is a profitability killer. These situations are not your fault as a dentist. The human body changes. Man-made objects break. Nature happens. You needn't be saddled with the cost of "retreatment" for the rest your patient's life.

Steps can be taken to reduce the chance of needing retreatment.

- Never accept anything from the lab with which you are not 100% happy.

- Temporize large restorations before permanently cementing them.
- Get parental and patient consent that they are happy with the result of orthodontic treatment before taking off the braces. Have the patient sign an agreement that they understand that if retainers are not worn, teeth will move.
- Take final photos and maintain records on every completed case.

EXPENSIVE EMPLOYEES

*There is only one thing worse than training
employees and losing them,
and that's not training them and keeping them.*
—Zig Ziglar

The most expensive employee is the "nice" employee who makes costly mistakes. Because they are friendly and agreeable, you feel that there is no valid HR reason to dismiss them. Yet, they may be costing tens of thousands of dollars to your practice. They may fail to collect payments or not enter contracts into your electronic billing system. They do this unknowingly, with a smile. They do not collect for services rendered. "Will that be cash, check, or credit card today?" is not in their vocabulary when they are seated at the front desk. They feel sorry for patients having to pay for your care. They sympathize with financial duress and agree with every patient excuse not to pay. They "train" your patients to expect "special arrangements," deferring collections for as long as possible (if ever), rather than asking for payment.

Expensive employees also make vital mistakes in bookkeeping. They may double-pay payroll, payroll taxes, or other accounts payable. You may be double-paying invoices and receiving refund checks in the mail. At some point, you feel that you can no longer trust this employee. You then hire an expensive investigator to audit your accounts, checking everything that this staff member did at your front desk. In addition to wasting your time and money, the expensive employee costs you peace of mind.

In dentistry, we often have a shortage of business-minded job applicants. Consequently, we spend thousands of dollars on consultants and training. Even then, many employees can't deliver. There is a disconnect between what they say they will do and what they actually do. They start making excuses for their performance. They push back telling you, "You're too hard on me," or "Don't 'micro-manage.'" These are cop-out excuses. These particular workers want to lie low and do as little as possible. Your office goals are not their goals.

Tasks can always be done by someone else for less cost, less training, and less worry. It just takes you, the doctor or business owner, to take action and make a change. In the end, the employee on whom you just spent an exorbitant amount of money in development training over many years may even quit. Then you must start all over again or take action yourself.

When you do find that talented, loyal, and capable employee, treat them like gold. That person will stick with you for the long run and be an office leader, someone on whom you can count. Such individuals are a rare find. When you have been given this golden opportunity, show your appreciation as much as you possibly can.

Chapter 19

SUCCESS

What have you done today, to help you reach your goals?
—Brian Tracy

Ultimate success includes removal of stress from your life. Stress can be created by uncertainty. Uncertainty produces fear. Taking action and completing the treatment coordination tasks that need to be done will give you a sense of accomplishment and well-being. Action produces momentum. Momentum produces engagement of those involved in its processes. Progress is your greatest motivation and winning is contagious.

ACTION

Action is the process of doing. It's not thinking, and it's not planning. It's implementation of the tasks that need to be done. It's doing the leading measures which produce the lagging results. It's execution of the work which needs to be done. If you want to achieve success, you have to take action.

In his book, *Traction: Get a Grip on Your Business*, Gino Wickman describes the inability to execute as the greatest weakness in most organizations. Why the difficulty? There are two factors: lack of discipline, and fear of conflict. Let's examine and eliminate both.

Eliminate Lack of Discipline

There are many forms of a morning huddle. I conduct a private daily huddle during my drive into the office each morning. I call my early morning receptionist/scheduler/financial coordinator during my morning commute. The coordinator and I review the schedule and other office matters in need of discussion or accomplishment that day. We exchange ideas and set a to-do list. This discipline extends to every management system, including what is done daily, weekly, monthly, and annually.

Daily Actions

We start the team huddle fifteen minutes before the first patient arrives. It is usually brief and run by the front desk scheduler. The day is reviewed, specifically looking for open appointments and overbooked or difficult periods. Each team member focuses on her own column of patients. The financial coordinator then makes note of monies due that day that need to be collected from the patients being seen.

The morning huddle ends on a positive note in an energized way. This is the purpose of a sports team huddle. It is a moment to collect your thoughts, gain control, and boost morale in a "Let's go!" kind of way. It reminds us of our necessary actions and that we are all in it together as a team. Then, the minute the office officially opens, we are prepared and ready to roll. We're warmed up! Each of us knows what we accomplish today counts.

Weekly Reflections

There is no better time to review the arc of progress than at the weekly team meeting. The process of "everyone rowing in the same direction" is built by a culture of clear expectations. You may want to call this your "weekly accountability meeting."

Face it. You are not going to accomplish much in the ten-minute morning huddle. To review reports and strategize for the future, one solid hour of uninterrupted time is required. Beyond strategy and progress, this is a time of bonding. It's a time to be heard, for each team member to express themselves, and a time for them to know and feel that what they do counts.

Keep food out of working meetings. Once food is introduced, attention goes to the food ("mayo or no mayo?"), and not to the topics at hand. Like any Fortune 500 company board meeting, a dental office strategy session needs everyone's undivided attention.

At the weekly meeting, each team member outlines performance as reflected by results. The review can include:

1. Production
   a) Month to date
   b) Year to date
2. Collections
   a) Month to date
   b) Year to date
3. A/R
   a) 30+, 60+, 90+
   b) Insurance A/R
4. Treatment Coordination
   a) Exams month to date
   b) Exams year to date
5. Conversion Rate
   a) Month to date
   b) Year to date
6. Referrals
   a) Year to date starts by referrer

The weekly meeting helps everyone to focus on their next **now**. We all need to focus on what we are going to do **today** after the weekly meeting is done. Many daily **nows** produce the success for next week, month, and year. Reporting action items can be assigned to specific team members and tracked on a white board.

Keep your meeting on the same day at the same time each week. Ours is Thursdays from 12:00 to 1:00 p.m. After the meeting adjourns, we break for lunch on our own, out of the office, to decompress. We resume seeing patients at 2:30 p.m. and work until 6:00 p.m.

We also don't answer incoming calls during this protected time. Our recorded message states that we are in a team meeting and will return calls at 1:00 p.m. Calls can be transferred to an answering service if you want to avoid missing any new patient calls during this hour.

A printed agenda will help ensure meeting clarity and efficiency. Give each team member the opportunity to speak in an uninterrupted fashion.

Go around the room twice so that everyone can express their ideas. On the first round, focus on the results of KPI. On the second round, discuss projects and new brainstorming ideas. I always like to ask "What are your hopes? What are your dreams?" Ending on a positive note, I usually share some inspirational thoughts from a book I may have read that week. This week, I reviewed the summaries from three short books written by Og Mandino listed in the bibliography of this book. Then I end by asking the team to anonymously grade this week's meeting on a scale of 1–10. This gives me a sense of how everyone is feeling about our progress and teamwork.

Monthly Analysis

The best way to predict the future is to create it.
—Abraham Lincoln

The first weekly meeting of the month gives you the opportunity to ask, "So how did we do last month?" Analyze your progress. How do we compare to the previous month and this same month during the past two years? What is the forecast for the future?

Results can be made apparent for all to see. An underperforming team member may not feel good about their report. They may even quit. Let them. When this happens, you have the opportunity to hire someone more capable of getting the work done, to reassign the job to someone else, or to do it yourself. You will likely improve results and overall office satisfaction by practicing this method of transparency.

Quarterly Review

The quarterly meeting is usually done with your accountant. It includes an in-depth review of profitability and finances. You have most likely accomplished at least a few of your project goals. After ninety days, it's time to change things up and move on in order to stay fresh and excited about the work at hand. Review and set new priorities quarterly.

ANNUAL PLANNING AND GOALS

The annual meeting is held off-site. Everyone is primed for reviewing, planning, and thinking outside the box. The doctor or manager as leader will prepare the agenda and themes of focus for the coming year.

Our team's annual "advance" (as we call it, rather than "retreat") is a highlight of our practice year. Team members prepare presentations, share ideas, and envision the future. We celebrate the successes of the past year and acknowledge everyone's individual efforts and achievements. We take time for appreciation and gratitude. Then we plan new projects and focus on what lies ahead.

In preparing for your annual meeting, you may want to ask each team member to answer three questions:

1. What did you think was our office's greatest accomplishment for the last year?
2. What was your personal greatest accomplishment in the office during the past year?
3. What are your expectations for our annual advance?

In this supportive environment, you may want to ask your group to discuss out loud: "What is this team member's greatest strength? What is this team member's greatest opportunity for growth?" This is great feedback that can both encourage and improve individual and overall performance. Next, each team member can be given the chance to describe at least one thing that they will do differently in the coming year to make the practice more successful.

Take time at your annual advance to fill out and discuss your SWOT analysis: strengths, weaknesses, opportunities, and threats. Issues revealed in this exercise can be tackled at the weekly meetings throughout the coming year. Take time to reflect on your vision, core values, mission, and tagline, as well as your practice's one-, three-, and ten-year goals.

Have lunch together at the annual meeting. Seize the opportunity to rejoice, to build trust, to get to know each other better, or to just blow off steam. This is a busy day of intense thinking and visioning. It is vital for team health and longevity. Being off-site together is a treat in itself. For a moment in time, the external world is held at bay. You've worked hard all year. Kick your heels up and savor what you've accomplished. Plan your future course to success!

ELIMINATE FEAR OF CONFLICT

Working hard for something we don't care about is called stress.
Working hard for something we love is called passion.
—Simon Sinek

When you introduce the radical candor of accountability at weekly meetings, there will be initial pushback. Some eyes may roll. There may be late adopters. There may be complainers. There may be denial. You may hear team members grumble, "We don't have time for this." **Stick with it.** Don't turn back. Carry on with courage, communication, and candor to accomplish your office goals. Not everyone will survive the culture of accountability that you institute and work hard to maintain. Not everyone will produce results. Not everyone will Take Action on what needs to be done.

You may have individuals who have been perfectly comfortable in their positions for years. They like the way things are; they are happy with low standards. Their salary is acceptable. And, they don't want to change. They don't want any new challenges. They are complacent.

But one individual's inaction can pull down an entire office. It can make everyone work twice as hard to gain a new patient to make up for the lack of performance of the inactive team member. They are simply keeping a seat warm and blocking an opening for a capable individual. They are not the right person, in the right seat, on the right bus. They are not ready, willing, and able. Be open to the possibility of turning an obstacle into an opportunity. The benefits of daring to change may surprise you.

MEETING FEEDBACK

The secret of change is to focus your energy,
not on fighting the old, but building the new.
—Socrates

At the conclusion of your meetings—whether the daily huddle, weekly, monthly, or the annual advance—take a moment to have your team members anonymously score the meeting on a scale of one to ten. Be open to feedback on how the gathering went and how it could be improved. Have all of those present turn in the anonymous paper. Evaluate the meeting yourself. How did you feel during the meeting? Did you start on time and end on time? Was it organized? Was it lively? Did everyone participate?

When I get evaluations for my meetings, I know that if I receive an average of nine or higher, it was a good meeting. At this level, everyone is engaged, fired up, and feeling optimistic about the future. If I get a result of seven or below, I know that I may need to supply a little motivation, give help or encouragement, perhaps reassign tasks, or pay more attention to the time. People may want to coast, they may be discouraged about our progress, they may think that things are just fine when in fact they are not. Be open to whatever constructive criticism you receive. Your meetings can only get better.

YOUR ACHIEVEMENTS

The path to success is to take massive, determined, actions.
—Tony Robbins

In June 2018, my team and I enjoyed our first bonus of the year. We had studied key performance indicators (KPIs) at our annual advance off-site meeting, overhauled job descriptions, completed annual reviews, and focused on bottom line outcomes via analysis of data of office metrics.

On the last day of the year, I went over our December production. More than a year had passed since we started our treatment coordination improvement journey. It had been a tough but gratifying time. Our engine previously had not been running at full capacity. Our new patient exams were up. Our schedule was better organized. Our collections were up. And our production for December was up more than 100% over the previous year.

During this time of taking treatment coordination action, I took over follow-up calls for pending, will call, exam no show, observation recall, and patients who contacted to reschedule. Exams seen over two years ago were placed into will call status, and the Will-call list winnowed down. Recall exams with no appointments were also phoned. I reached out to observation recall patients without scheduled appointments. As prospects started coming back in for appointments, motivation rose, and optimism grew. The patients were appreciative of the added service and our Google five-star reviews increased.

Everyone on the team engaged in the treatment coordination process. We added SymplConsult and always asked patients, "Would you like to get started today?" Our conversion rate doubled over the year before and quadrupled over two years.

I also personally started contacting accounts receivable. Statements were sent with pink "friendly reminder" stickers. A few families past 120 days were sent to a collection agency. The number of patients owing money fell to the lowest in our practice's history.

The day sheet was checked every evening and I also confirmed checks deposited into the bank each night. Everything was in order. We were functioning well on all gears.

An ambitious, energetic, registered dental assistant working in our office for several years volunteered to become the new treatment coordinator. She was able to complete same day records and same day starts. Patients signed up for care. Excitement built. Our engine was once again running smoothly. We knew where we were going. All gauges were on, and we were all flying together in the right direction.

IMPLEMENTATION

The key to success is action,
and the essential in action is perseverance.
—Sun Yat-sen

In an office of accountability, the doctor/owner must have a system for individual performance review. Some people will get A's and feel great about the job that they are doing. Some people will receive lower grades. If performance is measured, failing team members will either improve or quit.

Training and development of your team will not cure all of your management problems. Remember, that this isn't about "feel-good" seminars, attending conventions, or throwing parties. Accountability is hard work. It can also be expensive. But the opportunity cost of not training or keeping the wrong person in any given position is far greater than the expense of coaching or team development.

Jeff Palmer, CEO of the Case Acceptance Academy, states that when he is called into a dental office to improve treatment case acceptance techniques, fifty percent of the staff he encounters are not trainable because they do not have the capacity to do the job they were hired to do. The reason may be expectations were not clear. It may be that they needed additional resources to fulfill their role. By not diagnosing this problem, sub-par performance exists.

Some hires will catch on quickly. But one who cannot accomplish a given task after training and three attempts should be considered unfit for the position. An outside consultant may be able to identify shortcomings in your practice. You may need to hire a coach to help you with this process. Sometimes a doctor cannot see the hump on their own back.

Chapter 20

REFERRALS

*Do what you do so well that they will want to
see it again and bring their friends.*
—Walt Disney

When the treatment is done, how will your practice be memorable in the mind of your patient? If you want to know the answer to this question, you need to ask your patients yourself. Give them a customer service survey and ask the all-important question: "How likely is it that you would refer a friend or a family member?"

The entrepreneur asks, "How will my business look to the customer and how likely are they to refer others?" When patients compliment you for a job well done, take this opportunity to thank them and ask for referrals. Have ready access to a "Refer a Friend" card, brochure, or business cards that you can hand to your satisfied customer right then and there. This is not a time to be humble. Let your practice light shine!

PATIENT REFERRALS

*Loyal customers, they don't just come back,
they don't simply recommend you,
they insist that their friends do business with you.*
—Chip Bell

203

When your treatment coordination process is complete, and your results are beautiful, the highest success that you can achieve is to have your patient refer another patient.

There are five things that you can do to increase referrals:

1. Always provide excellent first-class care.
2. Ask for referrals every day.
3. Make referral cards readily available.
4. Give your patients logo-branded marketing items.
5. Support your patient's activities in the community.

COMMUNITY REFERRALS

Community referrals come from patient events, the internet, and all printed material and public relations efforts. Get out of your office and meet people. Bring lots of business cards with you and give them to your team members to distribute in their communities. Encourage your team to wear their uniforms and apparel displaying your logo, whenever appropriate. Make office promotion a team sport.

Sponsor events involving patients active or prominent in your community. Evaluate cost per contact ROI. For example, avoid settling for having your office name simply listed as having supported a sporting or charitable event. Insist that all donations be coupled to promotional material, to get your office name in the hands of potential new patients.

Take center stage in the community. The broader your reach, the better. Keep in touch continuously with historically good referral sources that have produced new patients, and be on the lookout for new opportunities.

DOCTOR REFERRALS

Staying in constant communication with fellow dentists and physicians will keep your office top of mind. Keep track of the number of doctor calls, lunches, and mailings you make each month. If you are a specialist, taking great care of your patients and sending them back to their dentist for follow-up care will complete the treatment coordination cycle of oral health.

A newsletter is a great way to keep in touch with referring dentists. An endodontist in my community puts out a newsletter each month. It includes news from the office, recipes, doctor message, and "case of the month," which I especially enjoy. This doctor makes root canals interesting!

Personally, I love taking my fellow dental colleagues out to lunch and getting to know them. Never eat alone. Getting to know your colleagues can literally double your referrals if you are a dental specialist. The dental community is constantly changing, now faster than ever before. Mature dentists are retiring and young dentists are moving in. New corporate practices are also becoming new landlords and managers. There's a lot going beyond advances in dental care. By the time you get through your dental colleague lunch list and share new developments, it will be time to start all over again!

Stay in Touch and Stay Visible

I wonder if you could help us to help other patients?
—Ashley Latter

Getting out of your office and active in the community can make your practice a household name. Make it a monthly goal to complete new actions via phone calls, writing a blog, posting on social media, and making office visits. All of these activities boost your profile and presence in your community. If you need more ideas on actions you can take to keep your practice visible, check out my book, *It All Starts with Marketing: 201 Marketing Tips for Growing a Dental Practice.* It includes a sample twelve-month marketing plan.

Always Say Thank You

Always take time to say thank you for referrals. Do it in writing. Do it right away. This thoughtful and effective action should not take you more than a few minutes. Tom Hopkins, the nation's number one sales trainer, states in his book, *How to Master the Art of Selling,* that spoken thanks are nice but rarely bring in more new clients. A handwritten thank-you note with your card motivates your referral source to send yet another referral. Hopkins advocates carrying three-inch by five-inch cards to fuel your gratitude machine. He personally sends five to ten thank you notes every single day.

Sometimes you actually might not know the specific individual in any given office who sent the referral. Have your best office PR representative "love bomb" the referring office by making a food run of appreciation. Then take the doctor/owner out to lunch. Personal attention is the best gift of all.

INTEGRITY

> *Happiness is when what you think,*
> *what you say, and what you do*
> *are in harmony.*
> —Mahatma Gandhi

When our values, thoughts, and actions are in alignment, we are at peace. Integrity is walking your talk. Integrity requires purposeful and intentional choosing. If everyone on your team believes, understands, and acts as if you are all connected, the entire office will be working together toward a common goal. All will embody success and the will to win. Take time to ask: "What's true? How does what we do affect all of us?" Communicate honestly. Be truthful and address office problems with a moral and ethical lens.

We will not be able to live our practice values and achieve results in isolation. We need to have everyone on board. Integrated management requires people with diverse backgrounds to together share the same life journey. Vulnerability is an asset. Admit when you need help. Listen to each other to foster solutions in a spirit of collaboration.

SYSTEMS

We have now completed the treatment coordination process, which includes: prospecting for new patients, engagement, influencing a "yes" decision, qualifying, conversion of case starts, performance, delivery of services, and finally, referral of new patients.

Give this process time. It will take at least ninety days to implement all these ideas and up to two years to fully reap the benefits. I hope that I have convinced you that having a system of treatment coordination is the key to running a successful dental practice. The title of the person who manages the system doesn't matter—the system matters. Over time, your organizational efforts will become automatic and a pleasure to be celebrated.

As the leader, you will no longer need to ask for things to be done. Office metrics will be proudly presented by team members who are "all in."

One sure constant is that you will need to do the work to bring about needed change. You will need to manage your team, conduct meetings, start cases, collect money, and all of the other things that go into running a successful small business.

TURNOVER

When you are a good person,
you don't lose people, they lose you.
—Joann Uolamo

Not every basketball player is good for the full-court press. Not every team can win the championship. Sometimes it's necessary to recruit new talent. Productive change may include staff turnover.

Not everyone can graduate high school, community college, college, dental school, or specialty training. Not everyone is organized or can run computer software systems or implement new technology. Not everyone will complete business management curriculums or even read this book. But you did. You want to build a successful office culture of accountability like the one you live on a daily basis. You've worked hard to establish your dental practice. You deserve to work in a great work environment with a mission-oriented team that will grow the practice, serve the patients, and support everyone working together, including you. As the leader and practice owner, you are entitled to having a winning team with unbridled enthusiasm.

In his book, *The Energy Bus*, Jon Gordon describes the words needed to dismiss what he calls "an energy vampire." Hopefully, this does not describe anyone in your office. Just in case it does, here is a dress rehearsal of what you may someday need to say:

"I can't have you on the team if you are going to prevent us from achieving our goals. I can't have you be a disruptive influence any longer. I'd rather have fewer team members and a team that is "all in," moving in the same direction and striving for the same goals, than a team with someone who has your work ethic and attitude. Your performance and track record give me no other choice. You are no longer needed here. Today is your last day. We wish you the very best."

For employees who don't want to be held accountable, let them go. No need to talk them into something they are not interested in doing. Let them find a new job with less accountability. Let them go to the dental office that doesn't ask for a reference. Let the next office deal with their baggage.

Some individuals may choose to leave dentistry altogether. This is not your concern. Business management is serious and challenging. In a small office, one team member can be twenty percent of your work force. Each employee is crucial to the success of your dental practice. Don't take separation personally. Dentistry is not for everyone.

THE MARSHMALLOW TEST

In a TED talk, Conor Neill describes the characteristics of a successful person. He asks, "Who would you bet on?" A well-known predictor of success is the Marshmallow Test. First conducted by the Psychology Department at Stanford University, children aged three to four were placed in a room and given a single marshmallow. They were told "This marshmallow is yours. If you do not eat the marshmallow during the next fifteen minutes, you can have another." Some children in this study think and think and think, staring at the marshmallow while pondering their choices. Others dive right in and eat it.

The fifty percent who delay gratification and don't eat the marshmallow qualitatively and quantitively do better in life as compared to the kids who could not resist temptation. This test of self-control has been found to be highly predictive of success in life.

Marshmallows don't work on adults, but the lessons of this study do apply to you and your team. Both need self-control. You as the dentist are likely to remain committed. You're in dentistry for the long haul. Your team members may have different motivations. When you assign tasks while you are away, how many employees can make it through even a three-week period of self-control? Not all. Those who can pass the Marshmallow Test will get the job done even when no one is looking. Others will be surfing the internet and looking for another job that pays a few more dollars per hour more. Then, when you return, they will try to extort you for higher pay. You will be dealing with this behavior your entire dental career.

In life and in business, loyalty is reciprocated and lack of loyalty is shunned. You will face job hoppers, negativity, and lack of performance issues. Failure is marked by bad habits. Be prepared to deal with them.

Success is characterized by repeated good habits. These people are not easy to find but they do exist. Reward those who take action and persevere. These winning individuals are the ones with whom you need to share your practice life.

YOUR SUCCESS

Winning is not a sometime thing; it is an all the time thing.
You don't win once in a while; you don't
do things right once in a while;
you do them right all of the time.
—Vince Lombardi

Dental practice management is serious business. It's not about having fun, attending meetings, or playing in a rock band. Practice management is taking action. The topic of treatment coordination may be dry, but every dentist needs to know and master the basics of running a successful practice. Office success depends upon hiring talented people of high character; clarifying objectives, mission, and vision; and training in processes and procedures. When done well, employees are empowered to make decisions. For teams that can't master treatment coordination, it's always Groundhog Day. It's back to retraining.

Positive outcomes lead to increased trust and autonomy. The doctor then is less likely to need to seek management oversight. Leading a team capable of carrying out functions correctly is every dentist's dream. Practice management is an integral part of dentists' careers. For private practice owners, it occupies at least fifty percent of our energies. We've got to get it right. Our ultimate financial success depends upon business management acumen.

I hope that the concepts in this book will help you make excellent practice management decisions for you and your practice. Mastery of dental practice management skills helps dentists feel fulfilled in their career dreams as well as sleep well at night. This leads to work happiness, low levels of stress, and better relationships with the team, the patients, and your family. This goal and the belief in the possibility of improved dental practice management have inspired me to write this book and share my own treatment coordination journey with you.

Happiness is gained from making a difference in your patients' lives. At Gorczyca Orthodontics, our vision is "Smiles change lives." When this aspiration becomes a reality, everyone has a great day. For me, success is epitomized by the following patient's thank you note:

> Dear Dr. Gorczyca,
>   Thank you for the excellent care that you provide and for creating an environment in your office that is happy, cheerful, and therapeutic. You are the best!
> —Jemila

It is my hope that you will also be fulfilled by your personal journey of continuous and never-ending improvement. Stay focused on your plan. We're all in it together, this wonderful thing called dentistry. Every day there is a new challenge—and an opportunity to take action for success.

CONCLUSION

Success is turning knowledge into positive action.
—Dorothy Leeds

By now, some of you are saying, "Hey, I could do that." Yes you can! Make things happen. Take action to start implementing changes needed to improve your treatment coordination systems. Remove chaos from your dental practice. Replace it with discipline, order, planning, and growth. Treatment coordination processes require a leader and that leader is you.

Still and all, why bother?
Here is my answer:
many people need desperately to receive this message:
I feel and think much as you do,
care about many of the things you care about,
although most people don't care about them.
You are not alone.
—Kurt Vonnegut

You now know that you are not alone in facing the daily challenges that you encounter in running a dental business. Treatment coordination is perseverance. It needs organization to be able to follow-through. It takes persuasion. Treatment coordination is sales success.

While running your dental business and employing people to get the job done, know that your work matters because your patients are counting on you, and they need your services. It is up to you to tell them what they need, to deliver care, and to solve their dental health problems. The treatment needs to be done so it might as well be done by you! Your works matters and you matter. When you take action, your patients start getting the dental care that they deserve.

We can do no great things, only small things with great love.
—Mother Teresa

I hope that this book has inspired your pursuit of treatment coordination excellence, and that it will contribute to your professional development, financial success, and professional happiness.

Take time now to fill out your own Treatment Coordination "Take Action" Calendar, which follows in Appendix 1. Use Appendix 2 as a guide. Start with those systems that need the most work in your office. For the sake of your patients, team, community, and especially yourself: Take Action—now. Here's to your success!

Appendix 1

TREATMENT COORDINATION TEMPLATE

	Engagement	Conversion	Delivery
Jan			
Feb			
Mar			
Apr			
May			
June			
July			
Aug			
Sept			
Oct			
Nov			
Dec			

Appendix 2

SAMPLE TREATMENT COORDINATION CALENDAR

	Engagement	Conversion	Delivery
Jan	I. New Pt. Calls	Pt. Postcards	XI. Tx Time
Feb	Referral Thank You	V. Ex/Start CR	XII. A/R
Mar	II. Total Exams/Mos.	E Mail Special	XIII. Insurance Aging
Apr	Pt. Welcome Cards	Text Messages	XIV. Pt Rx
May	Referral List	VI. Calls/Day	XV. CS Score
June	III. Calls/Ex CR	Dr. Reports	XVI. Pt. Rx Mo.
July	Welcome Folders	VII. Pending List	A/P Budget
Aug	Team Wall of Fame	Community Event	XVII. Comm. Rx
Sept	Patient Walls of Fame	VIII. Missed Exams	XVIII. Dr. Rx
Oct	IV. Same Day Starts	December Special	XIX. Starts/Month
Nov	SymplConsult	IX. Missed Obs.	XX. Meeting Score
Dec	Refer a Friend Cards	X. Will Call List	Annual Planning

*Roman Numerials indicate reports for review

ACKNOWLEDGEMENTS

A man of knowledge chooses a path
with heart and follows it.
—Carlos Castaneda

B ooks are built over time. I write to share the knowledge and experiences that I needed to improve systems in my own practice. Writing for me has been a personal labor of love, a quest to create dental resources, and document wisdom-gaining events. This book is the result of thirty years in clinical practice, collating experiences, conversations, classes, and collaboration with my colleagues and friends who care about orthodontics, dentistry, treatment coordination, dental practice management, and each other. Thanks to all of you for sharing your thoughts, experiences, and time with me.

I am grateful to the people who made this book possible. Thank you to the treatment coordination team at Gorczyca Orthodontics, without whom patient care and case conversion would not exist: Jolene, Lyndsay, Gwen, and Jessica. I greatly appreciate your hard work and dedication to our patients and practice.

Thank you to my dear friend, Dr. Maureen Valley of Valley Orthodontics in San Rafael, California, who was my classmate at the Harvard School of Dental Medicine and Harvard School of Public Health. Your passion for dental practice management and organization of the Practice Management Course at the Arthur A. Dugoni School of Dentistry, University of the Pacific gave birth to first a lecture, then a presentation, then my books. I owe you a debt of gratitude for the opportunity and inspiration you gave to me.

An enthusiastic thank you to one of my best friends, Debbie Seidel-Bittke, CEO of Dental Practice Solutions. You encourage and uplift everyone in the dental community. Your enthusiasm for hygiene and all things dental practice management are contagious. Thank you for our evening commute phone conversations and Friday afternoon practice management "happy hours."

A very heartfelt, deep thank you to Aimee Muriel Nevins of Fortune Management. We have been on a journey together first as rep-doctor, then as patient-doctor, followed by coach-client, and now as colleagues and friends during the creation of this book. Thank you for everything we shared and for being a model dental professional.

Thank you, Nancy Hyman, Manager at Hyman Orthodontics and CEO of Ortho Referral Systems, for your enthusiasm, and amazing editorial comments. Your dedication to the business of orthodontics is infectious!

Thank you, Jill Oslin Allen, for your friendship and feedback. Your experience and no-nonsense approach to contemporary orthodontic practice management is refreshing.

Thank you to Wendy Askins for your insight into cash-flow management systems, reports, and embezzlement. Your services at Prosperident are vital to every dentist in practice. It is a comfort having you as a colleague in the dental profession.

Thank you to orthodontist Dr. Maryann Kriger for your tireless work in the area of inventory pricing control. Your service, OrthAzone, has added a new level of cost control, organization, and awareness of inventory in our practice. Thank you for your support in the creation of this resource for dentistry.

Thank you to Kim Bleiweiss of Grasshopper Mouse Inventory Control Systems for reminding us that it's not just what you produce and collect that leads to financial success, but also what you keep after inventory expenses that make you a financially successful dentist.

Thank you to Dr. Robert M. Pick for your enthusiasm in service to your colleagues in all things dental. I appreciate your support and insight from the field of periodontics.

Thank you, Lisa Mergen of Ascendant Dental Development, for your contributions to dentistry in the area of leadership and coaching. Your understanding of dental team dynamics and doctor experiences and behaviors is truly insightful.

Thank you to Dr. Christopher Phelps of Phelps Institute for your outstanding contributions to dentistry in the areas of call tracking and influence. Your endless contributions as well as your positivity are admired and appreciated.

Thank you to Jeff Palmer, CEO of the Case Acceptance Academy, for your online interviews, videos, and insights into the dental treatment coordination sales process. You are a great resource for every dental professional.

Thank you to my publisher, Stephanie Chandler of Authority Publishing, for your assistance and advice in the writing of this, my fourth book. It is always a pleasure to work with you. Thank you for helping me to make my dream a reality.

A special thank you to my sister, Dr. Diane Gorczyca Patrick, for her edits and contributions from the field of medicine. Your dedication to proofreading this manuscript was a labor of love and highly appreciated.

A special thank you to my loving husband, Richard, for his brilliant editorial work, which has helped to complete this project and make it a success. All of my love to you and young Richard, for sharing my writing adventures every step of the way with curiosity, patience, and love.

Thanks to all of you who have purchased this book and read it to the end. I hope that you have learned from my experiences and that the events and concepts contained on these pages will help you in your dental practice. Thank you for your five-star reviews on Amazon. Your encouragement inspires me to "Take Action" and to continue learning, implementing, and writing about dental office management principles and best practices. Thank you from the bottom of my heart.

Ann Marie Gorczyca, DMD, MPH, MS
The Sea Ranch, California

ABOUT THE AUTHOR

A friend may be waiting behind a stranger's face.
—Maya Angelou

D r. Ann Marie Gorczyca is a frequent speaker. She teaches at both the University of California San Francisco and University of the Pacific Dental Schools, where she lectures on dental practice management to the orthodontic residents. Treatment coordination is the fourth lecture of a six-part series that also includes marketing, teamwork, customer service, treatment coordination, human resource management, and management systems.

Dr. Gorczyca is a Diplomate of the American Board of Orthodontics, a member of the Angle Society of Orthodontists, and a graduate of Advanced Education in Orthodontics (Roth Course). She is a member of the Seattle Study Club, the American Association of Orthodontists (AAO), the Pacific Coast Society of Orthodontists (PCSO), the California Association of Orthodontists (CAO), the American Dental Association (ADA), the California Dental Association (CDA), and the Contra Costa Dental Society. She was an orthodontic associate of Dr. T. M. Graber in Evanston, Illinois. She has worked in a multi-specialty group practice in Fairfield, California, and she has been a practicing orthodontist in Antioch, California, for thirty years.

Dr. Gorczyca graduated from Wellesley College, the Harvard School of Dental Medicine, the Harvard School of Public Health, and Northwestern University. She has studied at the Harvard School of Public Health's Department of Health Management and Policy, and she holds a master's degree in Public Health. She is active in her local dental community Seattle Study Club chapter. She has served on the AAO Council of Communications and the ADA National Boards Part II Test Construction Committee. She has served as a Board Member for the Pacific Coast Society of Orthodontists. She is president-elect, program chair, and sponsorship chair of the Northern California Edward H. Angle Society of Orthodontists and serves as sponsorship director for The Angle Orthodontist journal.

Dr. Gorczyca is the author of the books, *It All Starts with Marketing: 201 Marketing Tips for Growing a Dental Practice; Beyond the Morning Huddle: HR Management for a Successful Dental Office;* and *At Your Service: 5-Star Customer Care for a Successful Dental Office.* She was a speaker at the 2011, 2012, 2014, 2015, 2016, 2017, 2018, and 2019 AAO Annual Sessions and will speak again in 2021. She is a frequent presenter at the Ortho2 User's Group Meetings and spoke at the first Mother of Pearls Orthodontic Conference. She has spoken to her local dental society and at the Arizona Western Regional Dental Convention as well as many orthodontic state associations and alumni meetings. She lives in Walnut Creek, and The Sea Ranch, California, with her husband and son. This is her fourth book.

BIBLIOGRAPHY

Anderson, Mac; and Feltenstein, Tom. *Change is Good, You Go First.* Sourcebooks, Inc., Naperville, Illinois, 2015.

Anderson, Mac. *You Can't Send a Duck to Eagle School.* Sourcebooks, Inc., Naperville, Illinois, 2015.

Asulin, Gavriel. *Turn Your Dental Practice into a Successful Business.* Zameret Books, Israel, 2018.

Bard, Sherran Strong. *Successful Practices.* Tate Publishing & Enterprises, LLC., Mustang, Oklahoma, 2015.

Baron, Eric. *Selling.* DK Penguin Random House, New York, New York, 2009.

Beckwith, Harry. *Selling the Invisible. Business Plus.* New York, New York, 1997.

Blanchard, Kenneth. *The One Minute Manager Meets the Monkey.* HarperCollins Publishers, New York, New York, 1989.

Boothman, Nicholas. *Convince Them in 90 Seconds.* Workman Publishing Company, Inc. New York, New York, 2010.

Boothman, Nicholas. *How to Make People Like You in 90 Seconds.* Workman Publishing, New York, New York, 2000, 2008.

Burg, Bob. *Endless Referrals.* McGraw-Hill, New York, New York, 2006.

Chase, Landy. *NO to Lost Cases.* Landy Chase, MBA, CSP www.yestotreatment.com, USA, 2014.

Cialdini, Robert B. *Influence, Science and Practice.* Pearson Education, Inc. Pearson/Allyn and Bacon, Boston, Massachusetts, 2009.

Cialdini, Robert. *PRE-SUASION, A Revolutionary Way to Influence and Persuade.* Simon & Schuster, New York, New York, 2016.

Covey, Stephen R. *The 8th Habit.* Free Press, a Division of Simon & Schuster, Inc., New York, New York, 2004.

Coyle, Daniel. *The Culture Code.* Bantam Books, Penguin Random House LLC, New York, New York, 2018.

Dalio, Ray. *Principles.* Simon & Schuster, New York, New York, 2017.

Dobbs, Randy. *Transformational Leadership.* Parkhurst Brothers, Inc., Little Rock, Arkansas, 2010.

Doerr, John. *Measure What Matters.* Portfolio/Penguin. New York, New York, 2018.

Duhigg, Charles. *The Power of Habit.* Random House LLC, New York, New York, 2014.

Farran, Howard. *Uncomplicate Business.* Greenleaf Book Group Press, Austin, Texas, 2015.

Galante, Donna. *It's All About Millimeters.* 3L Publishing, Sacramento, California, 2013.

Gerber, Michael, E. *The E-Myth Revisited.* HarperCollins Publishers, New York, New York, 1995.

Gitomer, Jeffrey. *Little Red Book of Sales Answers.* Prentice Hall, Upper Saddle River, New Jersey, 2005.

Gitomer, Jeffrey. *Sales Bible.* Harper Collins Publishers, New York, New York, 2008.

Goldstein, Noah J.; Martin, Steve J.; Cialdini, Robert B. *Yes! 50 Scientifically Proven Ways to Be Persuasive.* Free Press. A division of Simon & Schuster, Inc. New York, New York, 2008.

Gorczyca, Ann Marie. *At Your Service.* Authority Publishing, Gold River, California, 2017.

Gorczyca, Ann Marie. *Beyond the Morning Huddle.* Authority Publishing, Gold River, California, 2015

Gorczyca, Ann Marie. *It All Starts with Marketing.* Authority Publishing, Gold River, California, 2013.

Gordon, Jon. *The Energy Bus.* John Wiley & Sons, Inc., Hoboken, New Jersey, 2007.

Gordon, Jon. *The Power of Positive Leadership.* John Wiley & Sons, Hoboken, New Jersey, 2017.

Gunn, Susan E. *Money In, Money Out.* Brainstorming Publishing, Arlington, Texas, 2018.

Halvorson, Heidi Grant. *9 Things Successful People Do Differently.* Harvard Business School Publishing Corporation, Boston, Massachusetts. 2012.

Hannabarger, Chuck; Buchman, Rick; and Economy, Peter. *Balanced Scorecard Strategy for Dummies.* John Wiley & Sons, Inc., Hoboken, New Jersey, 2007.

Harnish, Verne. *Mastering the Rockefeller Habits.* Gazelle, Inc. USA, 2002.

Harris, David. *Dental Embezzlement.* Tellwell Talent, Halifax, Canada, 2019.

Hatch, Laura. *Step Away from the Drill.* Dental Rock Star Publishing, San Diego, California, 2017.

HBR, *Guide to Performance Management.* Harvard Business School Publishing Corporation, Boston, Massachusetts, 2017.

HBR, *On Emotional Intelligence.* Harvard Business School Publishing Corporation, Boston, Massachusetts, 2015.

Heath, Chip; and Heath, Dan. *The Power of Moments.* Simon & Schuster, New York, New York. 2017.

Herbinko, Mel. *Wait! What? We're Growing!* Melissa Herbinko, USA, 2018.

Hopkins, Tom. *How to Master the Art of Selling.* Grand Central Publishing, Hachette Book Group, Inc. New York, Ne 2w York, 2005.

Horstman, Mark. *The Effective Manager.* John Wiley & Sons, Inc., Hoboken, New Jersey, 2016.

Hubbard, Elbert. *A Message to Garcia.* USA, Best Success Books, USA, 2013.

Jameson, Cathy. *Collect What You Produce.* Cathy Jameson, PhD., Davis Oklahoma, 2019.

Jones, Phil M. *Exactly What to Say, The Magic Words for Influence and Impact.* Page Two, Canada. 2017.

Keller, Gary. *The ONE Thing.* Bard Press, Austin, Texas. 2012.

Killeen, Addison, DDS. *By the Numbers.* CreateSpace Independent Publishing Platform, USA, 2018.

Latter, Ashley. *Don't Wait for the Tooth Fairy.* authorHOUSE®, UK Ltd., San Bernardino, California 2013.

Latter, Ashley. *YOU are Worth It.* authorHOUSE®, UK Ltd., Bloomington, Indiana, 2014.

Long, Weldon. *Consistency Selling.* Greenleaf Book Group Press, Austin, Texas, 2018.

Lynch, Kelly. *10 "Knows" to get to YES!* eAssist Publishing, Platinum Practice Solutions, 2018.

Maggio, Rosalie. *How to Say It.* Prentice Hall Press, New York, New York, 2001.

Mandino, Og. *The Greatest Miracle in the World.* Bantam Books, New York, New York, 1975.

Mandino, Og. *The Greatest Salesman in the World.* Bantam Books, New York, New York, 1968.

Mandino, Og. *The Greatest Salesman in the World Part II: The End of the Story.* Bantam Books, New York, New York, 1988.

Marr, Bernard. *Key Performance Indicators for Dummies.* John Wiley & Sons, Ltd. Chinchester, West Sussex, United Kingdom.

McChesney, Chris; Covey, Sean; and Huling, Jim. *The 4 Disciplines of Execution.* Free Press, New York, New York, 2012.

Michalowicz, Mike. *Profit First.* Portfolio Penguin, New York, New York, 2017.

Moffet, Dr. David. *How to Build the Dental Practice of Your Dreams,* Advantage, Charleston, South Carolina, 2015.

Nottingham, Alex. *Dental Practice Excellence.* All-Star Dental Academy, Plantation, Florida, 2016.

Peter, Laurence J. Peter, Hull, Raymond. *The Peter Principle.* HarperCollins Publishers, New York, New York, 2009.

Phelps, Christopher. *How to Grow Your Dental Membership Plan.* Christopher Phelps, DMD, CMCT, Charlotte, North Carolina, 2016.

Pryor, Angus. *The Dental Practice Profit System.* www.anguspryor.com, Australia, 2018.

Ries, Al. *Focus.* HarperCollins Publishers, New York, New York, 1996, 2005.

Schiffman, Stephan. *Selling When No One Is Buying.* Adams Business, Avon, Massachusetts, 2009.

Short, Justin; Maloley, David. *Titans of Dentistry.* Made in the USA, San Bernardino, California, 2019.

Sinek, Simon. *Leaders Eat Last.* Penguin Group, New York, New York, 2014, 2017.

Sobczak, Art. *Smart Calling.* John Wiley & Sons, Inc., Hoboken, New Jersey, 2013.

Stack, Jack. *The Great Game of Business.* Crown Publishing Group, Penguin Random House LLC, New York, New York, 1992, 2013.

Stein, Jr., Alan. *Raise Your Game.* Hachette Book Group, New York, New York, 2019.

Tracy, Brian. *Bull's-Eye, The Power of Focus.* Sourcebooks, Inc., Naperville, Illinois. 2015.

Tracy, Brian, Arden, Ron. *The Power of Charm.* AMACOM, American Management Association, New York, New York, 2006.

Wickman, Gino; and Boer, Rene. *How to Be a Great Boss.* BenBella Books, Inc., Dallas, Texas, 2016.

Wickman, Gino, and Paton, Mike. *Get a Grip.* BenBella Books, Inc., Dallas, Texas, 2012.

Wickman, Gino. *Traction.* BenBella Books, Inc., Dallas, Texas, 2011.

Wickman, Gino, Bouwer, Tom. *What the Heck Is EOS?* BenBella Books, Inc., Dallas, Texas, 2017.

Williams, Bill. *Marketing the Million Dollar Practice.* SEGR Publishing LLC, Grapevine, Texas. 2013.

Williams, Bill, *The $10,000 a Day Dentist.* Breezeway Books, Plantation, Florida. 2017.

Wilson, Larry; Wilson, Hersch. *Play to Win!* Bard Press, Austin, Texas, 1998.

Ziglar, Zig. *Secrets of Closing the Sale.* Revell, Baker Publishing Group, Grand Rapids, Michigan, 1984, 2003.

INDEX

OTHER BOOKS BY
DR. ANN MARIE GORCZYCA

Printed in the USA
CPSIA information can be obtained
at www.ICGtesting.com
LVHW021405120424
777240LV00033B/577